SAS
ESSENTIAL
SURVIVAL

SAS
ESSENTIAL
SURVIVAL

Barry Davies BEM

LEWIS
INTERNATIONAL, INC.

First published in the United States in 2001 by
Lewis International, Inc.
2201 NW 102nd Place # 1
Miami
Florida 33172
USA
Tel: 305 436 7984 / 800 259 5962
Fax: 305 436 7985 / 800 664 5095

First published in 2001 by
Virgin Books
An imprint of
Virgin Publishing Ltd

ISBN 1-930983-10-7

Designed by Design 23, London
Printed and bound in Spain by Bookprint, S.L., Barcelona

Contents

When I was a young soldier, about to join the SAS, I read a book called *The Long Walk* by Slavomir Rawicz. It recounts the trials endured by six men and one woman who, after escaping from a Soviet prison camp in late 1939, walked from the Arctic Circle across the Gobi Desert and south all the way to India.

After 4,000 miles and 18 months four of them, including one American, survived. Their story instilled in me a never-ending thirst for all matters relating to human powers of survival.

The need to improvise in the Western world has diminished due to the easy availability of most items required to answer our every need. Food, drink, clothing and tools are cheap, commonplace items plucked from the shelves of any supermarket. The real need to improvise in the cause of survival is only faced by those who, by misfortune, find themselves in an isolated and uninhabited area. They may or may not have fellow survivors to assist them or to care for; either way, improvisation becomes the shopping basket, and the will to live the means of filling it.

We are creatures of comfort, with television, central heating and social amenities providing for our every need and appetite. In a survival situation these ever-present amenities will be replaced by perilous threats to life – pain, thirst, starvation, stress, loneliness, and boredom which may threaten the balance of the mind. In such a predicament the will to live must overcome the desire to lie down and give up. In order to do this we must look back at how our ancestors survived, and the lessons they learnt from nature.

In many cases, if the need to survive presents itself we should be well equipped. Clothing to suit the environment, shelter, sufficient food and water and communications are essential items for those venturing into uninhabited regions, or for soldiers operating behind the enemy lines. In the event of an accident, when individuals are thrust unprepared into remote and hostile surroundings, the means to survive can still be found. Survival skills are common sense, requiring minimal equipment, much of which can be improvised from wreckage or from the natural surroundings.

Survival has one simple rule: work in harmony with nature rather than trying to adapt it to modern-day urban expectations. Why build shelter if it is not cold and there is little chance of rain? Why carry water when surrounded by lakes and rivers? Animals have no tools, yet they build homes, find food, and survive.

This book is designed to provide a wide variety of information to cover every aspect of survival. It covers the basics that apply in any situation, in any terrain or climate. There is information on basic equipment, medical emergencies, shelter, fire, water, food, navigation, travel and rescue.

Adding the new developments in the world of survival to the vast amount that already exists has meant the curtailment of some subjects. These curtailments have been made in the areas of plant and animal food; and in the military aspects, given that servicemen and women are already familiar with basic techniques of camouflage and concealment which may be essential to their particular survival situations. Research for this book was carried out by visiting some of the world's best survival schools, in America, Europe and the Far East. Additionally, through the kind offices of BCB International Ltd of Cardiff, UK – the world's largest survival equipment manufacturer – and many other similar companies, this book displays the most modern survival equipment available both for civilian and military personnel.

Anyone venturing into an uninhabited and potentially hostile area should carry a survival pack. The contents of the pack should be dictated by the type of terrain you are entering, and should provide the means to protect life in the event of a survival situation occurring.

Escape and survival equipment is issued as a matter of course to military pilots and Special Forces units; but the development of specialist survival equipment for civilian use has also increased dramatically over the past decade. This equipment varies from the basic items supporting such 'global' techniques as making fire, constructing shelter, and navigation, to those varying items required for survival in specific terrain and climatic conditions.

An important factor is that every item included in a survival kit has to be of real use, and its usefulness must be judged against its size and weight. Ultimately, each item must increase your chances of survival in and rescue from situations in which you may initially have no other resources apart from the clothes you stand up in.

Fire

Candle A candle will prolong the life of your matches by providing a constant flame (as long as you can protect it from wind and rain); it will help start a fire even when the tinder is damp. Additionally, a simple candle provides light and comfort to your surroundings. Choose a candle made from 100% stearine, or tallow (solidified animal fats) – this is edible and may therefore serve as an emergency food (do not try to eat candles made of paraffin wax). The candle wax can also be used as a multi-purpose lubricant.

Flint & Steel Matches, if not protected, are easily rendered useless by wet weather, while a flint and steel will enable you to light countless fires irrespective of the conditions. The flint and steel is a robust and reliable piece of apparatus, but its usefulness is vastly improved when combined with a block of magnesium. Sparks generated by the flint will readily ignite shavings scraped from the magnesium block onto kindling materials.

Survival Kit

A survival kit could save your life. Whenever you embark upon any journey or activity where a survival situation might occur, make sure that you have a survival kit with you – and, most importantly, that it is on your person.

Each item must be evaluated for its usefulness and, ideally, its adaptability to different uses; make sure that the sole purpose of one item is not duplicated by another. Once you have decided upon your final selection, pack the items neatly in an airtight and waterproof container such as a metal tobacco tin, a screw-top cylindrical metal container, a waterproof plastic box, or a resealable polythene bag inside a sturdy canvas pouch. Whichever container you choose, once it has been packed with the relevant selection of kit for the particular conditions you face it should not be opened until needed.

The components of your survival kit should not be regarded complacently, as guaranteeing your survival without further initiative; the kit should be seen rather as a catalyst which kicks your personal survival skills into action.

Left: *Wind and waterproof matches.*

Above: *A flint and steel.*

Matches Ordinary kitchen matches will not be of much use unless they are made waterproof. This can easily be done by covering them completely with melted wax, or coating them with hairspray. Special windproof and waterproof matches can also be purchased; each match is sealed with a protective varnish coating, and manufactured using chemicals which will burn for around 12 seconds in the foulest of weather.

Tampon Due to the fine cotton wool used in its manufacture, the tampon has proven to be the most efficient tinder and fire-lighting aid. It works best if the white surface is blackened with charcoal or dry dirt first, as it accepts the sparks and ignites more readily. British RAF and Special Forces packs contain two tampons as standard issue. The cotton wool can also be used in medical emergencies to clean wounds.

Water

Water bottle; the newer types on the market come fitted with a built-in filtration and purification system – you simply fill them, and drink from them.

Condoms A non-lubricated, heavy duty condom makes an excellent water carrier when supported in a sock or shirtsleeve. The water must be poured in, rather than the condom being dipped into the water supply; shake the condom to stretch it as it fills up. Used in this way a condom can hold about 1.5 litres (2.6 pints). Condoms will also protect dry tinder in wet weather; and are strong enough to make a small catapult.

Water Purification The means of water purification come in a number of different forms, from tablets to pumping devices. For inclusion in a survival kit you are best advised to choose tablets (about 50), as they are light to carry and quick and convenient to use. One small tablet will purify about one litre (1.75 pints) of water, although it will leave a strong chlorine taste. Tablets cannot clean the water or remove dirt particles, but they do make it safe to drink.

Clothing & Shelter

Needles & Pins Several different sized safety pins should be included in any survival kit. They make good closures for makeshift clothing, or can be baited as large hooks to catch fish or birds. Large sailmaker's needles, such as a Chenille No 6, have a large eye which makes threading easier, especially if the hands are cold or if you are using thread improvised from sinew. They will also be able to cope with heavier materials such as canvas, shoe leather or rawhide. Another good use for a needle is as a pointer in a makeshift compass, although it will have to be magnetized first.

Parachute Cord Parachute cord is an extremely strong alternative to plain string, having a breaking strain of about 250 kilogrammes (550 pounds). It can be used for lashing shelter frameworks and many other necessities; and the inner strands of thinner cord also make good thread for sewing or fishing lines. A survival kit should contain a minimum of 15 metres (50 feet).

Razor Blades Hard-backed razor blades make useful cutting tools, for gutting fish, cutting sinew, or when making a weapon. Despite its small size, if used with care the blade will continue to cut for up to a month. Its life can be prolonged by not trying to cut materials which are obviously beyond its capabilities.

Survival Bag Loss of body heat potentially leading to hypothermia is one of the most commonplace but deadly threats encountered in a survival situation. A simple survival bag made of polythene protects the body from both wind and rain and minimizes the risk. Two bags separated by a layer of moss, bracken, grass, hay, etc, will form a basic sleeping bag. The survival bag also has many other uses, including an improvised rucksack, a waterproof layer when making a shelter, a solar still, and when extracting water from plants.

Wire Saw A good saw, similar to those issued to the military, is made of eight strands of stainless steel wire; it is capable of cutting through wood, bone, plastics, even metal. A wire saw can be used when cutting timber to make

Survival Bags

One or more strong polythene sheet bags, big enough to climb into wearing your clothing and boots, will provide you with:

• Protection from rain, wind, and hypothermia.

• The basis for an insulated sleeping bag or mattress.

• A shelter roof.

• The means of collecting water.

• The means of distilling water.

• The means to keep your clothing and kit dry when wading rivers.

• If brightly coloured, as ground signal panels to attract SAR aircraft.

A stainless steel wire saw will cut through most materials, including steel.

a shelter, and to saw precise notches when constructing traps and snares. (Due to the friction a wire saw may overheat – saw slowly so as to avoid this.) The saw can even be used as a snare itself, by passing the smaller ring at one end through the larger ring at the other to form a running noose.

Navigation & Signalling

Air Marker Panels Air marker panels can be made from any light-weight fluorescent material, although orange is the standard recognizable colour. It is advisable to carry a sheet two metres (at least six feet) square, which can either be folded into different shapes (see under Signalling, page 151), or split into three 30cm (12in) wide strips. Do not split the sheet until there is an absolute need to do so – e.g. you have spotted a search aircraft – as the whole sheet is useful for other functions such as a makeshift shelter.

Compass A compass provides the means to establish direction and position, the two vital elements if you are forced to travel or need to give your co-ordinates during rescue. A small button compass is designed primarily as an emergency escape and evasion tool for the military, its use being restricted to direction-finding only.

'Silva'-type compass.

The liquid-filled 'Silva'-type compass is more commonly associated with navigation by map, and together these offer the means of precise position-finding.

Flares & Smoke A wide variety of signal flares and smoke canisters are available on the market. If you decide to add them to your survival kit you would do best to choose a standard flare pack containing a launch pistol and nine different coloured flares. Although it is a good idea to know which colour is traditionally associated with which intended signal, firing any colour will attract attention. When firing the flares take great care that the launch pistol is aimed skywards. In a life-threatening emergency, flares can be used to start a fire.

Global Positioning System (GPS)

GPS is relatively new to the survival market, but its popularity is growing. This state-of-the-art instrument is a navigational aid capable of plotting your precise position on the surface of the Earth. This is obviously of particular value in the Arctic, where a normal compass can become erratic. However, GPS has certain drawbacks in most pure survival situations; away from any other power source it relies on batteries, making its usefulness short-lived.

The Global Positioning System (GPS) utilizing the network of navigation satellites in Earth orbit is of limited value in most survival situations; although it may allow initial positioning, in the absence of a power source its batteries do not last long.

Heliograph Modern heliographs are small, light, and easy to use. They operate by reflecting the sun's rays precisely towards aircraft or other rescuers. On a clear, sunny day their reflection can be spotted up to 30 kilometres (18.5 miles) away. It is a good idea to familiarize yourself with the operating instructions prior to any rescue attempt.

Radar-Reflective Balloon Radar-reflective balloons are not new to survival, but in recent years they have improved dramatically. The principle is to inflate a balloon made from a special foil which can be detected by search-and-rescue radar from ranges of up to 38 kilometres (24 miles). Some are tethered to a length of line and flown like a kite, while others are inflated by gas; the latter will stay aloft for up to five days even in strong winds.

Strobe Designed for military rescue situations, the strobe is a bright blue light which flashes with great intensity and can be seen many miles away. These are perfect for location at night or in the darkness of the Arctic winter. Although the strobe is waterproof, in cold conditions it should be kept close to the body to preserve the battery strength. The strobe should only be operated when the sound of a rescue aircraft is positively identified.

Survival Radio Although there are a vast number of survival radios on the market, some are limited in range and capabilities. If your work or pastimes often take you into isolated areas then you are well advised to carry a radio telephone which is capable of world-wide communications. In the event of any accident requiring the emergency services your chances of survival will be greatly enhanced. Many surviving parties have been successfully rescued by telephoning the emergency services directly. While most mobile phones will only work where there is an established network, communications are improving all the time as global satellite phones are introduced.

Watch Although not a direct part of your survival kit, a watch can be an excellent navigational aid – providing that it is of the analogue type, i.e. not digital.

Whistle Modern survival whistles are compact and can have a range of up to 1000 metres (5/8 mile) on a clear day. Its main usefulness is for localised communication, i.e. between members of the survival party, or when the weather is so bad that only surface rescue is possible. Every life-vest carries a whistle for location after a disaster at sea. In the same way, an injured and immobile person can signal their location on land.

Food

Emergency Food Food is not an immediate requirement in a survival situation, as the body can do without solids for several weeks before it starts to deteriorate. However, morale plays an important part in survival, and this can be lifted by maintaining some normality. Having the means to make a hot drink produces this normality. Any food pack should be kept to the minimum: two fuel tablets, two tea or coffee sachets, sugar, etc.

Emergency food pack. In most situations only the minimum of food items justify their bulk and weight in the survival pack.

All survival packs should contain basic fishing kit, which has a high usefulness-for-weight value.

Meat stock cubes contain salt and flavouring and make excellent hot drinks; they can also be used to flavour food from the wild.

Fishing Equipment A survival fishing kit should consist of the following basic components: five hooks (size 14 or 16), approximately 30m (100ft) of line, 10 iron or brass weights, and swivels. A float can be made from a cork (which when charred will also provide hand and face camouflage). If there is room, include a plastic, luminous lure, and a small fishing net.

Snares Purpose-manufactured snares work best, but if you cannot get these then carry at least 5 metres (16.5 feet) of brass wire from which they can be constructed. Next to a rifle, snares are perhaps the most effective way of catching game. Brass wire can also be used for fishing traces, and when building shelters, making bindings for snowshoes or improvised packs.

Knife

Along with your survival kit you should select a good knife. For many reasons this may be the most important item you carry; it is therefore essential to choose a knife of high quality which is best suited to your needs.

A multi-purpose 'Swiss Army' type knife.

There are several types of blade to be considered in this context, such as those found on pocket knives and multi-functional tools, and purpose-made survival knives.

Pocket knives range from the simplest single-bladed type to multi-bladed, multi-function knives. Whichever knife you choose, always carry it on your person as a matter of course. Single-bladed knives offer little more than a simple cutting tool. If you decide on a pocket knife you will be better off with a multi-function, 'Swiss Army' type. This will provide the survivor with a versatile range of tools, including scissors, saw and screwdriver.

Survival knives tend to be much larger than pocket knives and are usually carried in their own sheath. Most of the better knives have a sharpening stone in a pocket on the sheath, and many have a hollow handle or a pouch on the sheath in which a basic survival kit can be carried, although the nature and number of items in the kit will depend on the price of the knife model. A large number of relatively cheap, poor quality survival knives have flooded the market in recent years. These tend to have a weak point where the blade meets the handle, which is likely to fail when the knife is most needed. Check the knife's construction and any attached survival items carefully before purchase, and certainly before venturing into the wilderness.

Keeping a Sharp Edge

The knife is a vital survival aid; do not misuse it by throwing it into the ground or at trees. Keep it clean, and know where it is at all times.

A knife with a blunt edge is nothing more than a useless piece of steel. Granite or dark, hard sandstone are best for sharpening a blade. Find a flat piece the size of an open palm; rubbing two rocks together will produce an even surface. Wet the stone surface and work the blade edge over it with a smooth action, always working the blade away from you across the stone. At first use a clockwise circular motion over the surface, then an anticlockwise motion. Learning to sharpen a blade is a skill that can only be achieved through practice.

Grinding the blade at the correct angle will produce a long-lasting cutting edge. If your intended travel will involve a lot of cutting then you will be better off carrying a sharpening stone or steel with you.

The next step from the 'Swiss Army' knife is the multi-function tool such as the Leatherman or Gerber, whose increased size and length gives extra leverage and weight to its applications.

Multi-functional tools serve endless applications, from shelter building to making improvised clothing and travel gear. In a survival situation the multi-function tool is likely to prove more productive than an ordinary knife. The better-known names such as Leatherman and Gerber are well made and should last a lifetime. Most types include pliers, wire cutters, cutting blade, saw, screwdrivers and files. Because of its importance the tool should be attached to the body by a length of cord to prevent loss.

Survival Medical Pack

Knowledge of even basic first aid skills is a useful and valuable accomplishment in everyday life, but in a survival situation these skills take on immeasurable importance. Even when medical training and equipment are non-existent, it is always possible to save life if the priorities of first aid are administered.

It is important to put together a small emergency medical kit, based on your own personal medical skills. Obviously, if you are not trained as a medic, you should only include basic items, as detailed below.

Antihistamine Cream Antihistamine cream will soothe the severe irritation that insect bites or allergies can cause. Antihistamine tablets can be carried as an alternative, but beware – some cause drowsiness.

Antiseptic Potassium Permanganate crystals (see below) are easy to carry and provide an all round sterilizing agent, antiseptic and anti-fungal agent. A tube of general purpose antiseptic cream is also very handy.

Aspirin Aspirin will relieve mild pain and headaches and reduce a fever. Carry a strip of about a dozen soluble aspirin tablets.

Dressings Include at least one large wound dressing in your medical kit. As any soldier will tell you, always have it ready for immediate use. Note – the inside of a wound dressing contains cotton wool which makes excellent tinder, so make sure to retain all used dressings.

Electrolyte Drinks Most survivors will inevitably suffer from dehydration; this can occur in both hot and cold climates, and is mostly attributed to diarrhoea. While replacing fluid loss is the priority, body salts and minerals can also be replaced by adding an electrolyte drink.

Magnifying Glass In survival situations a magnifying glass is traditionally associated with fire-lighting by focusing the sun's rays on dry tinder; however, it is also useful for finding hard-to-see objects such as splinters and thorns. Short, sharp burns are also effective for removing leeches and ticks from the body.

Mosquito Repellent The chances of contracting malaria and other mosquito-borne diseases can be reduced if the correct precautions are taken. Anti-malarial tablets, as prescribed by a doctor, need to be taken; but it is just as important to deter the insects from biting you in the first place, so it is recommended that you include a mosquito/insect repellent in your kit.

Plasters Carry various sizes and shapes of waterproof plasters. Larger plasters are best, as they can always be cut down if necessary. Keep your plasters together in a waterproof sachet.

Potassium Permanganate A small tube of this crystalline chemical has many uses, and is carried in military survival kits. If mixed with a glycol-based substance such as anti-freeze it can be used to light a fire. A small amount added to water will make a sterilizing mouthwash, and a more concentrated mixture can be used to treat fungal diseases.

Surgical Blades Two surgical blades take up little space and are best left in their protective sterile wrapping. In use they can either be held between the fingers, or a handle can be fashioned from a small stick. Do not discard used surgical blades; sterilize them by boiling, and re-wrap. When a blade is no longer viable for surgery it will still make an excellent arrowhead.

Salt Salt is essential when travelling in tropical climates. Carry a small amount to make sure that the salt balance in the body is maintained. Try to reserve this resource for medical uses only and refrain from using it for culinary purposes. Salt water is also helpful in treating fungal infections.

Suture Plasters If you are unable to administer stitches, butterfly sutures will prove successful in closing small wounds.

The first task for any survivors is to establish the priorities for treatment of the injured. Casualties are usually sorted into categories. Those who require urgent assistance to prevent immediate death must obviously be given priority.

Anyone suffering from an asphyxia disorder will need immediate attention. Shock caused by major injuries and severe haemorrhaging must be assessed; after a major disaster many may be hopelessly injured and thus cannot qualify for immediate assistance. The task is to identify the injury and establish how long the casualty will live without assistance; and to decide if any assistance that can be given will prove beneficial.

Breathing

Check a casualty's breathing by placing your ear close to the nose and mouth and looking down over the chest and abdomen. If they are breathing you should be able to both feel and hear the flow of air, and to see chest and abdominal movement. If these signs of breathing are absent, immediate action must be taken.

Check that the airway is clear.

First make sure that the airway is clear:

Tilt the casualty's head back gently while lifting the chin with the other hand. Doing this will automatically open the airway, and will also lift the tongue from the back of the throat so that it will not cause an obstruction. Supporting the head in the tilted position with a hand on the forehead, check inside the mouth for any blockage, e.g. dentures, vomit, etc. Gently remove blockages, without touching the back of the throat, as this may cause throat tissue swelling.

In many cases these actions alone may be enough to enable the casualty to breathe again. If this is the case, and they also have a pulse, then place them into the recovery position and maintain a periodic check on their condition.

Mouth-to-mouth resuscitation.

Any visible injury to the front or back of the head may also indicate that the casualty has damaged his neck or spine. In such cases maintaining an open airway will still be a priority over their other injuries. However, it is recommended that a collar or head support be improvised in order to keep the head properly positioned.

Artificial respiration If the casualty is still not breathing, you must get oxygen into their body. This can be achieved through mouth-to-mouth resuscitation, as the air we exhale still contains 75% oxygen.

LIFESAVER

The human body needs a constant supply of oxygen to function. If we stop breathing even for a few minutes the brain will start to sustain damage; the longer we go without air, the greater the damage. If casualties are unconscious, choking, or having trouble breathing, then they must be treated urgently.

In the case of an unconscious casualty, check for breathing and also for a pulse. If one or both are undetectable then emergency treatment must be given immediately. Urgent assistance must also be given to anyone who is choking or showing other obvious signs of breathing difficulties.

With the casualty's head still tilted back so that the airway is clear, pinch his nose to prevent air loss.

Breathe in deeply, and then seal your lips over the casualty's mouth. Gently blow into their mouth and watch for the chest to expand. It will take about two seconds for the chest to expand to its maximum capacity. Move your mouth away and wait for the chest to fall fully.

This should be repeated nine times before checking that the casualty's heart is still beating by feeling the carotid pulse point in the neck. It is no use providing the patient with oxygen if their heart is unable to pump blood to the necessary organs. If the heart has stopped, chest compressions (see below) must be administered.

In cases where mouth-to-mouth resuscitation is impossible or undesirable, e.g. when there is a serious lower jaw injury, mouth-to-nose ventilation may be carried out instead, but making sure that the mouth is firmly sealed first.

Artificial respiration should be carried out until the casualty is once more able to breathe unaided. Once the breathing rate is steady, place the casualty in the recovery position and monitor their condition every three minutes.

Chest Compression If the heart has stopped, it must be artificially pumped so that the oxygen carried by the blood can reach the vital organs. To do this a technique called chest compression is used.

Artificial respiration when there are two people available.

Before beginning this procedure it is vital to make sure that a pulse is entirely absent. If the heart is still beating, however weakly, then chest compression will cause damage.

Place the casualty flat on his back on a firm surface. Kneel beside him and locate the bottom of his breastbone – this is found where the bottom two ribs meet. Place the heel of one of your hands about three fingers' width up from this point; place your other hand on top of this, and interlock the fingers.

Lean forward over the casualty, making sure that your elbows are rigid and that your weight is pressing vertically on the casualty's chest. The breastbone should be depressed by about 4-5cm (2 inches). Release the pressure by leaning back, but without removing your hands. Chest compressions should be repeated at a rate of about 80 per minute, pausing for a pulse check every 15 compressions.

Generally, if the heart has stopped then breathing will also have stopped. In order for the casualty to have a chance of survival both artificial ventilation and chest compressions will have to be performed at the same time. If you are on your own, the correct procedure is to first give the casualty two assisted breaths, followed by 15 chest compressions. Continue with this cycle for one minute before checking on heartbeat and breathing.

If neither is present, continue with the alternated breaths/chest compressions until either the casualty's heartbeat is restored, help arrives, or you become too exhausted to continue.

Resuscitation by two people
If a second person is present and able to help, one should assist the casualty's breathing while the other manipulates the chest compressions. To begin with, four

While assessing your priorities, keep these rules in mind

❶ Do not panic, no matter how serious the situation. Panic means that you will think less clearly. Take several deep breaths to calm yourself.

❷ Each casualty's injuries will need to be assessed. You will need to use all your senses: ask (if the casualty is conscious); look (and if possible feel over the body for broken bones, blood etc); listen; smell; think – and act.

❸ Conscious casualties are an important source of information. Ask them to describe their symptoms and what they feel may be wrong with them.

❹ Avoid taking any action that will put you in danger. If you become injured, you will not be able to help anyone else.

❺ Boost the morale of your casualties. Offer bcomfort, reassurance and encouragement, thus building their mental strength and will to live.

❻ Get uninjured survivors to help you. Ask (out of earshot of any injured person) if anyone else has any medical experience.

❼ Separate those who are saveable from those who are not.

Attempt to remove any obstruction by slapping between the shoulder blades.

assisted breaths should be given followed by five chest compressions. Subsequently, the correct procedure is to give one assisted breath for every five chest compressions. There should be no pause between the end of the chest compressions and the beginning of the assisted breath.

After one minute check for pulse and breathing; if neither is present continue the alternating breath/compression cycle and check every three minutes. Continue until either heartbeat and breathing are re-established, help arrives, or both helpers become too exhausted to continue. If heartbeat and breathing do return, check for any other injuries and place the casualty in the recovery position.

Choking Choking requires immediate assistance, as the airway is blocked and therefore no air is getting through to the lungs. Choking can be recognized by the casualty suddenly being unable to breathe or speak, grabbing at their throat or their skin turning pale blue.

The first priority is to remove whatever is causing the blockage in the windpipe. If the casualty is conscious, get them to cough it up. If this does not work, check the mouth to see if the object can be cleared with a finger. If not, bend the casualty as far forward as possible, preferably so that the head is below the level of the lungs. Give five sharp slaps between the shoulder blades with the heel of the hand, and check to see if the obstruction has been dislodged. This is usually enough to remove the object, but if it does not work you will have to try to clear it by using abdominal thrusts.

Aiding a casualty who is choking.

To do this, stand behind the casualty and put your arms around him. Ball one of your fists and lock

The Recovery Position

An unconscious casualty with a regular heartbeat and who is breathing normally while showing no sign of serious injury should be placed in the recovery position. In this position the head is slightly lower than the body, thus preventing the tongue from blocking the airway and allowing any liquids such as blood or vomit to drain freely from the mouth.

Kneel to one side of the casualty and turn his head towards you. Straighten the nearest arm alongside the body, with the other folded across the chest. Cross the ankles and roll the casualty towards you. Gently bend the upper arm and leg so that they safely maintain the body in the position. Keep the head, neck and back in a straight line.

If the casualty has spinal injuries or wounds the position may have to be slightly modified. In such cases use improvised padding, such as towels or rolled clothing, for extra support.

it in place with the palm of your other hand, making sure that one thumb is pressing into the abdomen. Pull your hands sharply inwards under the casualty's ribs. Repeat up to four more times before checking whether the object has been expelled. If this does not succeed at first, give five more back slaps and then five more abdominal thrusts. Keep trying until the object becomes dislodged.

Choking when unconscious If the choking casualty becomes unconscious, first lie him on his side with his abdomen supported against your knee, and give four to five back slaps.

If this does not dislodge the object, turn the casualty onto his back, kneel astride him, and perform abdominal thrusts. To do this, locate the heel of one hand just below the ribcage and cover it with the other hand. Press sharply inwards and upwards with the heel of the hand, up to five times. Check in the mouth to see if the object has been expelled. Continue alternating back slaps with abdominal thrusts until the obstruction is removed. If the casualty begins to breathe normally, place him in the recovery position and check breathing and pulse rates every three minutes.

If breathing does not recommence and/or there is no pulse, start assisted breathing and, if necessary, chest compressions.

Self-help when choking If you find that you are alone and choking, find something like the back of a chair or a tree trunk, and push it inwards and upwards into your abdomen to expel the air and, hopefully, the blockage. You could also attempt to use your own hands made into a fist to achieve the same effect.

Pressure Points

Indirect pressure utilizes pressure points. These are found where arteries cross bones near the skin's surface. For survival purposes, concentrate on the four points which flow to each limb.

❶ The pressure points in the arm are found down the centre of the inner side of the upper arm, on the brachial arteries.

❷ The main pressure point in the leg is on the femoral artery. The pressure point for this artery is in the middle of the groin. It is often easier to locate if the knee is bent so as to create the groin crease. Press firmly at this point against the bones of the pelvis.

❸ Locate the pressure point and, placing the thumb or fingers on it, apply enough pressure to flatten the artery against the bone. This should stop the blood flow.

❹ Pressure must not be kept on for any longer than ten minutes, or else other healthy tissue will be damaged through lack of blood. While using indirect pressure the wound may be dressed more effectively; however, do not use a tourniquet, as this may cause tissue damage.

Bleeding

Once breathing and circulation are restored the next priority is bleeding. Bleeding may be external or internal. Internal bleeding is almost impossible to treat with first aid, but external bleeding can be controlled.

Wounds present two main problems. Firstly, extensive bleeding can cause shock to develop, and will, if not controlled, lead to death. Secondly, any break in the skin will let infection in, so it is imperative that the wound site be kept clean. There are three procedures to help stop the bleeding:

Direct Pressure Use a sterile dressing if you have one; if not, find a clean piece of cloth. Place the dressing on the wound and press on it gently but firmly. If you have no dressing available then you may have to use your hand, but bear in mind the dangers of infecting the wound. Use only dressings that are large enough to cover both the wound and part of the surrounding area. It is possible that the first dressing will become soaked through with blood. If this happens, lay a second dressing over the first and, if necessary, a third over the second.

Tying a bandage around the wound and dressings will keep the dressings in place with a continued firm pressure. It is important that the bandage is not tied too tight, as this will restrict the flow of blood to the whole area.

Some large wounds will tend to gape. If you have suitable dressings you may use these to bring the edges of the wound together; otherwise you may have to use your hand. Blood flow from a large wound may be stopped by applying firm pressure with a pad of dressings, to the site of the greatest bleeding.

Using pressure on the wound helps the body's own mechanisms to slow and finally to stop the bleeding. The damaged ends of blood vessels will shrink and start to retract in order to slow down the blood loss. Clotting agents are released so that the blood

Applying a Tourniquet

1 Use a loop above the wound secured with a square knot.

2 Insert a strong stick or similar under the loop to act as a tightening device.

3 Twist the stick, tightening sufficiently to stop bleeding.

4 Secure the stick to prevent the tourniquet becoming loose.

begins to thicken, and eventually forms a plug over the wound.

Sometimes these mechanisms will be enough to stop the bleeding on their own. However, the casualty may still be in danger of going into shock. It is therefore vital that they rest; and reassurance, too, is important – if the casualty is anxious it will only serve to raise his heart rate and blood pressure. An injured limb should be elevated above the level of the heart, as long as it is comfortable for the casualty and not liable to make any other injury worse. This elevation reduces the flow of blood to the damaged area and helps the veins to drain blood away, reducing blood loss. The elevated limb should be supported if possible, either by you or by padding.

Indirect Pressure If, due to the severity of the bleeding, the techniques described above do not work, then indirect pressure should be tried. However, this only works on arterial bleeding, so it is important to identify what type of bleed you are dealing with.

Arterial bleeding takes place from vessels which are carrying filtered and oxygenated blood away from the heart and lungs. It has

Fractures

1 Complicated fracture where broken bone has damaged blood vessel.

2 Open fracture where bone is exposed.

3 Closed fracture where bone is not exposed.

4 Secure fractured limb above and below the knee and at the ankle.

5 Use padding with foot injuries. Elevating the foot reduces swelling.

6 Support a broken arm with a splint improvised from rolled up newspaper. Never use metal splints in a cold climate. Immobilize the arm with a sling to speed recovery and avoid further injury.

no impurities and is therefore bright red. It will also spurt out of the wound in time with the heart-beat.

Venous bleeding takes place from vessels which are carrying blood full of impurities away from the tissues towards the heart and lungs to be filtered and re-oxygenated. As venous blood is low in oxygen it is dark red in colour. It runs steadily or gushes from a wound at a steady rate.

Tourniquets The aim of first aid is to save life. If the damage to a limb is so severe that it plainly requires amputation, or if part of the limb is missing, and direct pressure will not stop the bleeding, then you may need to employ the third procedure by applying a tourniquet.

The tourniquet can be made from whatever cloth is at hand, but avoid any thin material that will cut into the flesh. Place it around the extremity, between the wound and the heart, 5 to 10cm (2-4ins) above the wound site.

Never place it directly over the wound or a fracture. Use a stick as a handle to tighten the tourniquet, but tighten it only enough to stop blood flow. Clean and bandage the wound.

The tourniquet must be slowly released every 10-15 minutes for a period of 1-2 minutes; however, you should continue to apply direct pressure at all times. It must be stressed that applying a tourniquet to prevent blood flow is a dangerous procedure, and should only be attempted when all else has failed.

Fractures

Fractures normally occur during an accident in which a body has stumbled unrestrained or has been hit by a flying object. Not all fractures are readily apparent, but a casualty may have a bone frac-

A skull fracture or concussion must be suspected if any or all of the following symptoms are present:

1 An obvious head wound, a bruise or a soft or depressed area on the scalp.

2 Unconsciousness, even for a short period of time.

3 Clear or watery blood coming from the ears or nose.

4 Blood in the white of the eye.

5 The pupils of the eyes are unequal or unresponsive.

6 A steady deterioration in responsiveness to external stimuli.

ture if he has difficulty in moving a particular part of the body normally. The reason for a fracture is fairly evident, and it is followed by a sharp increase in pain when movement of the affected part is attempted. Pronounced swelling, bruising, distortion and tenderness at the site of the injury are also good indicators of a fracture. An injured limb may look deformed or shortened, and a distinctive grating sound may be heard while attempting to move the limb. Signs of shock may be evident, especially if the injury is to the ribcage, pelvis or thighbone. The casualty may also have felt or heard the bone break.

Splints can be improvised with composite materials as well as single objects.

In a survival situation the scope for treatment of a fracture is limited to immobilization of the injured part.

Splints should be applied before the casualty is moved unless there is some form of imminent danger which requires immediate evacuation. If conscious, fracture casualties will be experiencing pain, so handle them with the greatest of care so as not to cause increased distress. If the fracture has also caused a wound, this must be treated and stabilized before any splints are fitted.

Splints Suitable splints can be improvised from small branches, sticks, or suitable pieces of equipment; rolled clothing or bedding can also be used in an emergency. Make sure that the splint is padded and that it supports the joints both above and below the fracture. In the case of a leg fracture, if no suitable substitute for a splint can be found in your environment then immobilize the injured leg by tying it to the good leg instead.

Sometimes a fractured limb may become twisted, shortened or bent in such a way that immobilization proves impossible. Gentle traction to re-align the limb can be used as long as the casualty can tolerate the pain. Pull gently in a straight line with the bone until the limb has been straightened. If this is done properly the casualty may find that the pain and any bleeding at the site of the fracture are significantly reduced.

Once you have done all you can to straighten the limb, apply the splints. If possible, elevate and support the fractured limb as this will help to reduce both any swelling and the danger of the casualty going into shock.

Make sure that the casualty receives plenty of rest.

Open Wounds

Cleaning Open Wounds The purpose of washing a wound is to remove as much bacteria as possible, thus giving the body's own defensive system the best chance of finishing the job. All exposed wounds, no matter how small, need to be cleaned. This is best done with water which has been sterilized by boiling, but clean, pure drinking water will suffice if boiling is not possible.

Deeper wounds can be washed out more efficiently by making some form of irrigation device which will deliver a strong jet of water into the wound. A small plastic bottle or a polythene bag can be pierced with a pinhole so that the water jets out when it is squeezed.

Adding a very small amount of soap or potassium permanganate to the water will assist in flushing out the wound. The amount of potassium permanganate crystals added should be barely enough to tint a pint of water; similarly, only enough soap should be added to barely cloud the water. If in doubt, err on the side of weakness.

Debris and Foreign Bodies Before starting any cleaning or irrigation, open the wound to its fullest extent and examine for debris – bits of clothing, glass, dirt, or any other foreign body which may have been forced into the wound at the time of injury. If these are small and not deeply impacted, remove them; if no properly sterile instruments are available, wash your hands with soap and water

LIFESAVER

No matter what your situation, if you intend to handle open wounds or burns – whether on yourself or other casualties – you should reduce the risk of further infection by sterilizing your hands. Wash them with water, snow, alcohol, or anything that will disinfect them.

and use your fingers. (Instruments and wound dressings can be sterilized by boiling for five minutes.) Once the wound is open and foreign bodies have been removed, scrub it briskly while irrigating at the same time – this is a job best done by two people. Work quickly, as this will be very painful for the casualty. Once finished, apply a clean sterile dressing, and arrest any fresh bleeding by direct pressure. Check the wound on a daily basis.

Unless they are life-threatening, larger foreign bodies deeply impacted should be left in place, as pulling at them may cause more serious damage. Control the bleeding by direct pressure, squeezing the wound along the line of the foreign body. Next, form a padded ring which will fit neatly over the protruding object, and secure it with a dressing.

Sucking wounds If air io allowed to enter the lungs from puncture wounds to the chest or back then a sucking wound will develop. Always check for sucking wounds if missiles or debris of any form have penetrated deeply, or if a rib is protruding from the chest or back. The lung on the affected side will collapse, and as the casualty breathes in so the sucked air will also impair the efficiency of the good lung. If the condition goes untreated the result will be a lack of oxygen reaching the bloodstream, which could cause asphyxia.

If a sucking wound is suspected, immediately cover the area with your hand. Support the casualty in a lop-sided sitting position with the functioning lung uppermost. Cover the wound with a clean dressing and place a plastic sheet over the top so that the plastic overlaps the dressing and wound; tape it down so as to form an airtight seal. If a foreign body is present in the wound, do not remove it, but pack with a ring as described above and fit an airtight seal.

Dislocations

Dislocations are caused when bone joints become separated and get out of alignment. This can be extremely painful, as the nerves and blood flow are affected. The best way to relieve this pain is to re-align the joint as quickly as possible. Although this is a simple process the joint will be swollen and extremely

It is possible that you may become injured while you are on your own, and in this case it is sensible to have thought out a self-help routine:

❶ Try to rest. Lie down somewhere, but preferably out of the wind.

❷ Use direct pressure on your wound to control the bleeding. If possible apply a dressing, sterile or improvised.

❸ If available, use a bandage to maintain pressure. Tie it firmly but not so tight as to restrict circulation.

❹ If possible, elevate the injured part and support it.

❺ Pain will be lessened if you try to keep as still as possible.

❻ Try to make sure that you can keep warm.

Using a weight to assist reduction of a dislocation when there is nobody else available to help.

tender and the limb will suffer from a lack of mobility.

Dislocations are treated by reduction or 'setting' the bones back into their proper position. There are two basic methods available to the survivor, depending upon whether they are alone or not. In either case the appropriate action should be taken as quickly after the dislocation as possible. Both, if successful, will bring about a lessening of pain and restoration of the circulation. Once reduction is completed the limb should be immobilized, using splints if possible, and allowed to recover.

Use a well-padded splint above and below the injury site. Always check the circulation below the dislocation after completing the splint. Remove the splint after a week and start gentle exercises until the limb is fully functional.

Unassisted reduction The lone survivor will need to improvise some form of weight, e.g. a large rock or log, to which they can attach a cord from the limb. The idea is to stretch the limb slightly by countering against the weight, and aligning it back into place.

The procedure requires the body and/or limb to be rotated in order to set the joint while at the same time comparing it to the joint on the opposite side. All movement must be kept to a minimum, yet must be positive rather than hesitant.

The procedure should be performed lying down if possible, as it is extremely painful and the manoeuvre will require a great deal of will-power on the part of the survivor.

Assisted reduction The same basic procedure of stretching and re-aligning the limb is followed, but it has the advantage of being more often successful, since manipulation is usually more positive and precise when the casualty does not have to deliberately inflict pain on himself. Where possible one person should hold the casualty in a comfortable position while a second manipulates the limb into alignment. Again, this procedure is best done with the casualty lying down.

Concussion & Skull Fractures Skull fractures and concussion are also common after major accidents.

Concussion is a temporary disturbance of the brain, normally due to a severe blow or shaking. If conscious, the casualty should be made to lie down with their head and shoulders supported. If unconscious, make sure that they are breathing and have a pulse – if not, carry out artificial ventilation and chest compressions immediately.

If the casualty is unconscious but the breathing and pulse are normal, turn them into the recovery position and maintain a close check on their vital signs.

In either case, make sure that the casualty is kept warm and quiet and handled carefully. Apply a light padding to the injured area and hold it in place with a dressing. If blood is being discharged from an ear, lightly cover it but do not block it. Concussion is normally only a temporary disturbance from which the chances of recovery are good.

Burns

Naked flames, boiling water, electrical devices, friction, acid, liquid oxygen, freezing metal and the sun all cause skin burns. The severity of the burn and the amount of body area affected will determine the casualty's survival chances.

Cooling Burns caused by naked flame should be cooled immediately to limit the damage caused by heat to the skin tissues. Either pour cold water slowly over the affected part, or immerse it totally in clean cold water.

This should continue for at least ten minutes to stop further tissue damage and to reduce pain and swelling.

Dressing Once the burn has been cooled, a dressing should be applied immediately to limit the possibility of it becoming infected. Do not attempt to remove any charred fibres that have stuck to the burn, but remove any restrictive clothing around the site to prevent further swelling. The dressing should be sterile and made of a non-fluffy material. Avoid adhesive dressings, which will only aggravate the injury and cause more damage.

In a survival situation sterilization of cloths, bandages and dressings can be achieved by scorching the cloth with a candle, as this will kill most bacteria. Do not be tempted to burst any burn blisters which form, as these provide a protective layer. A solution containing tannic acid derived from boiling oak or beech bark can be used to clean the burn; make sure that any such concoction has cooled before using it. If polythene bags are available they can be used to cover the burnt limb and help stop further infection.

To reduce the possibility of shock setting in, lay burn casualties down and keep them warm and comforted. If the casualty is unconscious, turn him over into the recovery position and monitor his breathing and pulse closely.

Burns

1. Cool the burnt area by immersion in cold clean water, or fresh snow.

2. Protect hands and feet from further infection with a sealed polythene bag.

3. Do not use adhesive or fluffy dressings.

4. Do not break blisters or remove loose skin.

5. Do not apply ointment, oils or fats to the burn.

After the immediate priorities for first aid have been identified and acted upon, survivors in remote and uninhabited regions will face the need to monitor and safeguard their health under challenging conditions, perhaps for quite long periods.

In a survival situation it is obviously important to maintain health while awaiting rescue – and this is absolutely central to preserving the survivors' option to make an attempt at travelling across country themselves.

Personal Hygiene When ill, weakened or injured, the first priority is not medicine but a good standard of personal hygiene.

Proper hygiene, care in preparation of food and drink, waste disposal, insect and rodent control (and, of course, prior immunization) will greatly reduce the causes and number of diseases and infestations to which the survivor may fall victim. The importance of prevention of disease during any survival situation cannot be overstated, and physical hygiene is important if you wish to protect yourself.

If possible, wash daily with warm water and soap. A small amount of water can be used to sponge the face, armpits, crotch and feet at least once a day. Regular washing, especially after defecation, is a necessity no matter how bad you are feeling.

Eat as often as you can to keep up strength, but stick to simple, easily digested and nourishing foods – a vegetable soup is ideal. Make sure that your water is pure and that you wash food before cooking it. Raw food should be avoided as it is not only harder to digest in most cases, it is also a possible source of contamination. Make sure that your liquid intake is sufficient – water or a herbal tea is the best drink for a body in a weakened state. Although these points are common sense, they will aid the body to heal itself or to fight off an illness or infection.

Underclothing collects dirt and sweat, so keep it dry and clean, especially if you are unable to change it regularly. If clothing cannot be washed it should be shaken vigorously and exposed to the sun and air at least once a day. The sun is a useful agent against disease, as few bacteria or viruses can survive exposure to ultraviolet light.

Lice & Ticks Along with ticks, lice are also carriers of typhus, which is transmitted through their faeces.

Clothing should be checked regularly, and if any of these pests are discovered they should be removed either with a delousing powder if available, or by boiling,

Immunization

Vaccinations are available against many diseases which may be threats in a survival situation, including typhoid, paratyphoid, yellow fever, typhus, tetanus, cholera and hepatitis. It is essential to obtain as many vaccinations as possible, making sure immunization records are kept up to date. Prior to visiting any foreign country you are advised to seek current medical advice and take extra immunizations and precautions. Make sure that you carry a good supply of anti-malarial tablets where necessary.

or by exposure to direct sunlight for a few hours. Louse bites should not be scratched, no matter how irritating, as this leaves the skin vulnerable to infection with typhus through the louse faeces. Instead, wash the skin with weak antiseptic or a strong soap.

When a tick bites into skin it embeds its head in the flesh. For this reason they should never be simply pulled off, as they may leave the head behind and this will cause an infection. Smothering their bodies in smoke, iodine, paraffin, petrol, etc will only make them vomit – thus, again, causing infection. The best way to remove a tick is to pinch the surrounding skin with tweezers, pulling the tick with the flesh. Apply thumb pressure to the small hole and it will stop bleeding and soon heal.

The juice from crushed nettles mixed 50/50 with fresh water can be used as a body wash which will reduce lice infestation. The same concoction also makes an excellent shampoo for keeping the hair free of head lice.

Hair Hair can attract lice, and is best kept short. It is easier if another member of the party does this, using any available scissors rather than a knife. During any long-term survival situation (more than one week) all members of the party should crop their hair. Do not discard any cut hair – it can be used as tinder in fire-making. Shaving should not be encouraged during cold weather survival as it leads to cracked skin.

Teeth Teeth can be cleaned with an improvised toothbrush made by chewing the end of a stick to separate the fibres; use the stick only once, then discard it. Lye slurry, soap, sand and salt can be used instead of toothpaste. The inner strands of paracord or the fine fibres on the inside of tree bark can be used as dental floss. A mouthwash can be made from salt water, or pine needle tea. Painful cavities can be filled with candle wax to help relieve the pain. A compound of fennel and mistletoe will also reduce toothache.

Keeping the teeth clean reduces the risk of serious stomach upsets.

Feet Feet require constant maintenance; blisters or ingrown toenails can be extremely painful, and may prevent a survivor from walking. Foot blisters are usually caused by ill-fitting boots, poor quality socks or loose laces, combined with long periods of walking over rough, uneven ground.

Stop and treat small blisters immediately by covering them with surgical tape. A severe blister is often filled with fluid, and can be made more comfortable if the fluid is drained. Large blisters which look as if they are about to burst should be punctured with a sterilized needle and thread. Run

If you have to travel across country then how well you take care of your feet may be the factor which decides whether or not you survive.

the needle through the blister from side to side, then clip off the thread leaving a short length hanging out each side of the blister. This will ensure that the fluid drains without creating a large break in the skin. Make sure that the surrounding area is kept thoroughly clean and dry.

Ingrown toenails should be treated as soon as they become apparent. Without removing the nail the best method is to shave the top centre of the nail with a razor blade from your survival kit. Skim the middle third of the nail, shaving from the bed towards the nail tip. Place a thin piece of plastic under the nail to prevent accidentally cutting the toe. When the nail is thin enough it will buckle into a ridge and relieve the outward pressure. Removing the nail altogether should be avoided, as this will require a dressing and may prevent the patient from walking for several days.

Survival Soap

Good hygiene prevents disease and illness, and is never more important than in a survival situation. Survival soap is easy to make and will help clean wounds and wash clothes.

❶ Melt animal fat by cooking it in water while constantly stirring. Drain off the grease into a flat tray to harden (a metal wheel hub is ideal).

❷ Take a clean sock or shirt sleeve and fill it with cold, crushed ash from the fire; soak the whole sock in water, and hang it up so that the water and charcoal drip out – this liquid is potash or lye.

❸ Remelt the grease and add the lye, mixing two parts grease to one part lye. Boil the mixture until it thickens to the consistency of porridge, then allow it to cool.

❹ It can be used in its liquid form, but is best left to go solid and cut into blocks.

Diarrhoea

Charcoal powder can be purchased and added to your survival medical pack, or produced in the field when required. Small amounts can be taken dry, but it is best administered mixed with water into a slurry.

As with most foreign travellers, survivors will suffer from bouts of continuous diarrhoea. Although unpleasant they pose no threat to life, and the disorder is usually self-limiting. In the case of the survivor diarrhoea will normally develop as a result of consuming contaminated food or water, although malaria, cholera and salmonella produce similar symptoms.

Diarrhoea is detected when the number of daily bowel movements increases by a factor of two or more, the stools being soft and watery.

A small amount of charcoal slurry will settle the stomach, as charcoal absorbs toxins from the gut. Take charcoal from a cold fire, grind it to a powder and mix it with water. The thickness of the slurry is determined by its usage; for diarrhoea a light mix is required, about 10 grammes (0.35 ounce) of charcoal to a cup of water; for stomach poisoning the mixture should be 50 grammes per cup.

Herbal Medicine

Herbal medicine has been practised worldwide since before recorded history, and many modern medications are derived from refined herbs. Although many herbal medicines and ancient treatments are effective, they should only be used when medical supplies are not available. The subject of survival medicine would fill many volumes, but a few of the more popular methods and remedies are listed here. Most herbal medicines are mild in their effects and therefore quite slow-working, unlike today's powerful pharmaceutical drugs. They work with the body, encouraging its natural healing processes and strengthening the immune system. Most herbal remedies are safe to use, especially if the casualty is in a weakened physical state, and will not cause side effects. Any allergies to the herb will become apparent before any serious damage occurs. Bear in mind that not all plants have a positive effect; some plants with medical properties, such as foxglove, should never be used by the untrained.

Herbal medicines do not need to be complicated mixtures of different plants. Often one plant substance alone will have the desired healing effect. Try using one plant on its own and for a matter of days to register its effects.

Fluid loss

Fluids must be replaced using sterile (boiled) water mixed with a little salt. Check medical packs for any electrolyte powders. A juice made from potassium-rich fruit – such as apples and oranges – will help, as will honey if it can be found.

Safe Medicinal Plants

As with edible plants, medicinal plants should only be considered if they have first been positively identified. It is vital to know how to use the plant correctly. If the plant has a medical reputation but is also poisonous, leave it alone. The smallest mistake in dosage could kill. Potency will also vary in a plant from one location to another, so a correct dosage of a poisonous plant is almost impossible to judge in the wild. Plants that have an edible as well as a medicinal use are the best to use.

Making Medicines

Whether for internal or external use, clean fresh herbs and plants are required for medical purposes. Internal use will require the plant being prepared either by infusion, decoction, maceration or powdering. Infusion is simply a matter of pouring boiling water over the plant or plant parts and leaving them for around 5 minutes (a little longer if the plant is tough). Decoction means boiling in order to extract the most from the plant. Maceration means crushing the plants or plant parts and leaving them for several days in water. Powder is obtained by drying followed by crushing and grinding. The powder can be used to form a brew by adding water or moistened and rolled into small tablet-sized balls, the latter will be very strong. External use is either via a compress which has been soaked in a decoction or infusion and then applied to the wound, or a poultice made by crushing the plant or plant parts which are applied directly to the wound.

Aloe Vera This amazing plant can be used for a number of different ailments, from soothing bites, stings, and minor burns to calming fever. The gel-like juice is extracted by crushing, and can be used for external applications in its raw state. The gel can be partly sun-dried and thickened by continuous stirring, the resulting balm being used to heal most skin abrasions.

Aloe vera has a multitude of medicinal uses.

Fennel and Mistletoe To treat toothache, crush together an equal amount of fresh mistletoe leaves and fennel. Cover your finger with the juice and rub onto the gum. This was used in medieval times and is very effective.

Giant Puff Ball This large fungus should be cut into segments and rubbed into a powder. This can then be used on wet sores and weeping wounds. Cutting the ball into slices 3cm thick will produce a number of wound pads. Two hundred years ago puff balls were often harvested prior to battles purely for the purpose of field dressings.

Plantain Add fresh plantain leaves to the water when washing

Giant puffballs can be used to treat weeping wounds.

your clothes; this stops lice infestation. Lining your grass bedding with the same leaves will also help keep ticks and lice at bay.

Willow Willow provides the means to make an effective pain relief. Cut out a large patch of willow bark, making sure that the white inner skin is attached. Remove this skin in strips and boil it in clean water for about an hour. Allow to cool before drinking. Putting more of the inner skin into the concoction or boiling for longer can increase the strength. The stronger the brew, the less you need to take. The process involves trial and error, but this is an extremely effective remedy.

Garlic All members of the garlic family such as garlic mustard, chives, leeks and hedge garlic etc, can be used to treat a wide variety of ailments. As a general rule of thumb all those plants that smell of garlic when the root is crushed are part of the same family and safe to eat (if unsure carry out the edibility test). Garlic contains an antibiotic called allicine together with concentrates of vitamins A, B and B2. Eating garlic will help protect you against food poisoning, amoebic dysentery and typhoid. The plant root bulbs should be cleaned and the first layer of skin removed, thereafter they can be eaten raw or used to flavour soups and stews. Garlic can be consumed in large quantities without any side effects. The most common found is mustard garlic, the whole plant can be eaten.

Remedies

Antiseptics Wounds become infected quite easily, but there are certain plants which have natural antiseptic properties. If you have time, take the plant material and make an infusion with which the wound can be washed. In an emergency the same plant material can be chewed to make a pulp to be applied to the affected area. Some plants which may be used in this way are: selfheal (prunella vulgaris); greater plantain (plantago major); birch (betula pendula); dried burdock (arctium lappa), and thyme (thymus vulgaris).

Bites & Stings Apart from being irritating, insect bites, in particular, can leave the skin open to infection. Some insects are also the carriers of dangerous and debilitating diseases and parasites. It is important to be aware of the dangers and to take advantage

Remedies

Dock leaves.

Using crushed laurel leaves to soothe an itchy rash.

• The bulbs of wild garlic can be crushed and used directly on a wound, or may be boiled to extract the oils and applied as an antiseptic.

• A handful of salt added to a litre of boiling water and allowed to cool will produce a solution that will kill bacteria.

• Sphagnum moss is a natural source of iodine, and makes a useful dressing. It is found in bogs all over the world.

• Remove the paper and tip from a cigarette and chew the tobacco until your mouth has produced enough saliva to allow swallowing. The ingested nicotine will kill most stomach worms. Repeat the process for several days until the infestation has stopped.

• The addition of hot peppers to your food diet will create a parasite-free digestive system.

of the several lines of defence that are available.

Bee, wasp, hornet, spider and scorpion stings should be removed if visible and the wound dressed with a cold compress of mud. Slow-burning, smoky fires will drive insects away; it is best to light one on the windward side of camp. A ring of ash around your sleeping area or camp site will deter most crawling insects.

The pain of stings from plants such as nettles can be reduced by rubbing them with a fresh dock or burdock leaf.

Treatment with Maggots

There has been much speculation about the use of maggots in wound treatment. They do have a value; however, they can be a double-edged weapon, and their use must be carefully monitored. They should only be applied when antibiotics are not available. Despite the hazards involved, maggot therapy should be considered if a wound becomes severely infected and ordinary debridement of rotting tissue is impossible.

Maggot activity should be monitored closely.

❶ Remove any bandages to expose the wound to flies, which will deposit their eggs on the rotting flesh.
Warning: The flies are also likely to introduce bacteria into a wound, causing additional complications. Limit the number of flies accessing the wound – one exposure should ensure enough maggots. Live or hatching maggots will naturally find their way into the wound, at which stage the wound should be covered with a clean dressing.

❷ The dressing should be removed daily to check for maggots; if none are found within three days expose the wound to the flies once more. If there are too many maggots, remove the surplus with a sterilized instrument, leaving no more than a hundred in the wound.

❸ Monitor maggot activity very closely each day. The maggots produce a frothy red fluid which must be sponged away with a sterile cloth in order to keep track of the maggots' progress. The time taken by the maggots to clean the putrefying tissue from the wound will depend on several factors: the nature and depth of the wound, the number of maggots present, and the type of fly which layed the eggs.

❹ Many people believe that maggots will only feed on dead tissue, but this is not the case – they also eat living tissue if nothing else is available. Maggots eat at an alarming rate, so the wound should be checked on a regular basis or whenever the patient feels any sharp increase in pain; this, and any fresh blood flow, are good indicators that the maggots have eaten all the dead tissue and have started to invade healthy flesh.

❺ At this stage all the maggots should be removed by flushing the wound with sterile water or fresh urine; it should then be carefully sponged dry. The wound should be left open, and checked every few hours to ensure that it is completely free of maggots. Once all of the maggots are removed, bandage the wound and treat as normal.

Coagulants The body has remarkable powers to stop bleeding on its own but there are plants which can help. As they are rarely around when you most need them, collect them whenever you come across them, dry, powder, and store them. Useful herbs to stop bleeding include bistort (polygonum bistorta), yarrow (achillea mille-folium), shepherd's purse (capsella bursa-pastoris), horsetail (equise-tum orvense), and marigold (calendula officinalis).

Digestive Disorders The most common digestive disorder that a survivor may encounter is diarrhoea (see box on page 36). Fortunately there are many plants which have astringent properties helpful in easing this condition. Remember that any diarrhoea or vomiting will also deplete the body's fluid levels, so it is important that any fluid loss should be replaced. A simple infusion of the following herbs will replace fluid and administer medicine at the same time: blackberry leaves (rubus fructicosus); strawberry leaves (fragaria vesica); dog rose petals (rosa canina), and bistort (polygonum bistorta). Bistort root is recommended for severe cases of diarrhoea, such as in dysentery. Upset stomachs can be calmed by infusions of meadowsweet (filipendula ulmaria) or peppermint (mentha piperita).

Headaches Survivors often suffer from headaches, especially during the first few days of their ordeal. A good remedy is to drink soothing mint tea and apply crushed mint leaves to the forehead.

Other effective teas can be made from rose hips and/or petals, and feverfew (chrysanthemum partenium).

Mosquitoes As mosquitoes breed in stagnant, sluggish water or swampy ground you would be well advised to avoid camping near any of these, aiming for higher ground where possible. They bite mainly during the late evening and night – although those which carry dengue fever also bite in the daytime. Use any available insect repellent. Make sure that exposed skin is covered as much as possible; tuck trouser legs into socks and sleeves into gloves. Cover your body with mosquito netting, parachute material, handkerchiefs, or even smearing mud over any exposed areas of skin will reduce the number of bites that you will suffer.

Poisoning If you are forced to live on wild plants your chances of being poisoned are greatly increased. The danger can be averted by eating only those plants or fungi which are easily recognizable. If poisoning is suspected, the patient must be made to vomit. A glass of water mixed with salt followed rapidly by gagging should produce the desired result. Use you fingers or a smooth cold instrument such as a spoon handle to stimulate the throat. After vomiting give the patient a drink of charcoal slurry, to help absorb any remaining poison.

Stings from Sea Creatures

Sea creatures can leave painful stings which in some cases can be fatal, but generally they are short-lived.

Stings from sea creatures such as jellyfish, stingrays, weaver, lion and zebra fish can be extremely painful, while those of the Portuguese man-o'-war can also bring on paralysis and breathing problems. If any sea creature stings you, try to isolate the venom by placing a tourniquet between the wound and the heart. Don't worry about the length of time the tourniquet is applied – the venom is short-lived and it can be released after ten minutes.

Stings from sea creatures such as jellyfish and stingrays can be remedied with a mild acid such as lemon juice.

Use hot water on and around the wound area as this will help neutralize the venom, as will any form of mild acid such as lemon juice or vinegar. Use tweezers to remove any tentacles or spines visible in the flesh, do not touch with bare hands. Those patients who are having trouble breathing or who are unconscious due to a sting should be given mouth to mouth resuscitation and cardiac massage for a period of at least fifteen minutes as the venom is short-lived.

Rashes Avoid scratching any rash. Dry rashes should be kept damp and wet rashes kept dry. A small rendering of boiled animal fat and crushed charcoal rubbed into a dry rash will help prevent the skin cracking and promote healing. Fungal infections are best exposed to direct sunlight, and kept dry. Skin rashes that become infected should be treated as open wounds and dressed accordingly.

Malaria

Malaria is the world's most widespread disease; 300-500 million people are infected, and 1.5-2.7 million die of it each year. The vast majority of cases occur in the Third World, particularly in sub-Saharan Africa but also in Central and South America and all over Asia.

The parasites which cause malaria are transmitted by the bite of female anopheline mosquitoes. The parasites migrate to the victim's liver, where they multiply. After nine to 16 days they return to the bloodstream, breaking down the red cells and causing anaemia. At this point the outward symptoms appear: fever and chills, headaches, and joint pain. These symptoms may be mistaken for flu, food poisoning, or even jet lag. In danger regions, always assume that fever means malaria unless you have good reason to think otherwise. Untreated, plasmodium vivax can lie dormant in the liver for years, causing recurrent bouts of illness.

Treatment
For many years the drug chloroquine was an effective preventative; this is now true only in some areas of Central America, the Caribbean, North Africa and the Middle East.

Protecting Yourself Against Malaria

- Before travelling to danger areas, check which antimalarial drugs are recommended on the web site of the Centers for Disease Control at www.cdc.gov/travel.

- Take the drugs regularly throughout your trip.

- Follow all the advice in this book on avoiding mosquito bites: use repellents, smoke, etc; cover your skin; avoid stagnant water particularly after dark.

- Most antimalarial drugs should also be taken for four weeks after you leave a danger area.

- If symptoms strike after you leave the area – fatigue, weakness, light-headedness, fever, chills, nausea – get immediate medical help. Tell your doctor where you have been travelling.

Rabies

Rabies is a viral infection of the central nervous system, contracted from the saliva of infected animals – most commonly, dogs, cats, jackals, foxes, wolves, racoons, skunks, mongooses, bats, etc. Dog rabies is quite common in Central America, India, Nepal, Sri Lanka, Vietnam and Thailand; it is also found throughout South America, Africa, and the rest of Asia, and is not unknown in southern Europe.

Assume any bite suffered from a warm-blooded animal in the Third World is dangerous, even if the animal had no obvious symptoms (classically, drooling at the mouth coupled with agitated body movement and noises, and unprovoked aggression or over-friendliness).

In humans the symptoms are fever, headache, sore throat, nausea, loss of appetite, followed by pain or numbness at the infection site, skin sensitivity to temperature changes, depression and insomnia. As the virus attacks the central nervous system extreme pain is suffered when swallowing, leading to 'foaming at the mouth' through inability to swallow saliva, and terror at the sight of water (hydrophobia). Dementia or paralysis follow, and sometimes coma, always leading to death.

The great danger lies in the long incubation period between infection and the appearance of symptoms – this can vary from five days to more than a year in some cases, the average being two months. Once symptoms appear in the infected human there is no cure, and a very distressing death is inevitable. It is therefore vital to take strict precautions before and after suspected exposure.

Treatment
Pre-exposure vaccines are available, but immunization must be planned well ahead. A course of three injections is given over 28 days. Its effect may also be impaired if you are taking antimalarial drugs. Some individuals may be allergic to compounds in one or other of the three types of vaccine (RVA, HDCV and PCEC). For all these reasons, get qualified medical advice in good time.

If caught soon enough, rabies is curable during the incubation period, so treatment should always be sought even if some time has passed since the bite. If in doubt whether an animal which has bitten you is rabid, there may be some circumstances in which you can capture it and watch it to see if it develops (further) symptoms; handle it with extreme care to avoid further infection.

A rabid animal will normally become obviously sick within about three days of inflicting an infectious bite. If you are far from any realistic hope of post-exposure treatment, it will at least reassure you if the animal does not develop symptoms. If treatment may become available, cut off the animal's head and pack it carefully – its salivary glands can be tested when you reach help.

Having assessed your situation, you must judge the urgency of your need for shelter. This need will be particularly urgent in both hot and cold climates. Cold, wind, rain, snow, and exposure to the sun pose a major threat to survival.

Any type of forest area will provide the material to make a good shelter.

Apart from the last, all these factors can lead to the rapid development of hypothermia – which can kill long before the effects of any lack of food or water. Hot climates can also pose a danger to the survivor without a shelter, as too much exposure to the sun can cause overheating of the body and a loss of body fluids leading to severe dehydration, sunburn and sunstroke. Although the effects of heat upon the body are slower to inflict damage except in extreme desert conditions, without adequate protection they can still cause death.

Shelter Location

If you have a tent or commercially produced shelter then this should be used in preference to building a makeshift structure. If you do not have a tent, check whether the natural features in your surroundings might provide temporary shelter. Do not waste time and energy in building a shelter or windbreak if naturally occurring protection can be found nearby. Look at the possibilities afforded by trees, bushes or natural hollows. Caves and rock overhangs will also give shelter – but check for signs of dangerous rock falls.

The type of shelter you build, and where it is sited, will depend very much upon the terrain, climate and your personal situation but there are general guidelines which can be applied in any situation:

If there is no natural cover and you have to construct one from scratch, build it so that its entrance or open side is on the leeward side (i.e. facing away from the wind). A shelter on a hillside may be warmer than one on a valley floor, where colder air tends to sink; but a hillside location may also prove too exposed. The ideal shelter should be built close to a source of firewood and building materials in a wooded area, near a stream which contains fish.

Building Materials

Foliage Foliage, particularly if it is large-leafed, will make an excellent waterproof covering for a shelter, and should prove quite durable. Branches, bark, large-leafed plants, straw, moss and grass can all be used as a covering, while thin trees and saplings make excellent frameworks.

Snow used to anchor the edges of a shelter

Turf Trees and shrubs may be in short supply in some areas, e.g. flat, open grassland. In such a site turf can be used to construct shelters and to roof them over.

Rocks and Stones Rocks and stones provide very acceptable building material in places where the ground is too hard to dig or where a more permanent shelter is required. In many desert areas where there are few trees or shrubs, piled rocks provide the obvious means to make a quick shelter.

Snow, Sand and Mud Snow blocks can be cut and formed into a number of different shelters, and although not so easy to use, sand can also provide protection. Mud, when mixed with dry grass, straw and/or animal droppings, can be formed into practical sun-dried building bricks. Mud can also be used to fill cracks, insulate and prevent draughts.

Sheeting Plastic or canvas sheeting of any kind can be used in the construction of a shelter – ground sheets, parachutes, plastic sacks, jute sacking, tarpaulins and blankets can all be used in some way. Wreckage from vehicles and aircraft can all be put to use providing excellent weatherproof shelter.

Tree-line Areas

Forested areas provide many opportunities to make a shelter. Fallen logs offer the means to fashion an especially simple type. Move two fallen logs until they are close to one another and parallel; then dig a trough between them. Roof the area between the tops of the logs with branches and foliage. If there is only one log to hand, a low earth wall can always be thrown up to provide the second side of the shelter, or else it could be used as the basis for a small lean-to.

Lean-to The lean-to pattern of shelter is the most commonly built, and one of the simplest to construct.

Foliage used to provide additional insulation to a shelter.

The only important thing to remember is to build it so that the roof slopes down into the prevailing wind. The frame itself could be covered by any material that is available – plastic sheeting, foliage, a groundsheet, wreckage panels, etc. Turf blocks or layers of firm, dried mud on top of foliage provides an excellent cover – it is both waterproof and windproof, and will not blow away. Once the roof has been established, the sides can also be filled in using a similar mud, foliage or turf fabrication.

Construction time: 1 hour.

A shelter frame ready for thatching can be made even when long poles are scarce.

If you have a good supply of cord in your equipment, you could consider building a variation on this basic lean-to. This version is especially suited to areas with short, shrubby vegetation. First, cut four or five very long, pliable stakes, and push their ends into the ground in a circular pattern so that they will stand firm.

Bend the tops inwards at an angle of 45 degrees, and tie them together. If there are any suitable saplings growing in the immediate area, consider saving yourself some time and energy by incorporating them into the design as they stand – they will also give much more strength and stability to the shelter.

Once the basic framework is in place, weave twigs, branches and

Turf Shelters

1 Turf shelter built with two walls of blocks of different heights, to provide the roof with a run-off slope.

2 Even simpler shelter made from single wall of turf blocks and a lower earth wall.

foliage between the struts to form a rigid structure. Add more foliage until it is totally covered, and finally complete the roof with a layer of firm mud or light turf.
Construction time: 1 hour 30 minutes.

Quick Tree Shelter Any small tree can form the basis of a quick and simple shelter. After selecting the tree, cut or saw part way through the trunk at about shoulder-height. Once you have cut most of the way through, push on the upper portion so that it falls and rests on the ground while still being supported by the intact part of the trunk. Break the up-standing branches on the outside of the trunk so that they hang down and form the sides of the shelter. Cut out the branches from the underside to make room for you to get underneath, and weave them into the shelter's structure.
Construction time: 30 minutes.

Turf Shelter 1 If trees are in short supply or entirely absent and you are on grassland, it is still possible to build a shelter from cut turf bricks. Once the sides are built to the desired height try to find material to make 'rafters' to support a turf roofing layer; small sticks or boughs are ideal for this if any are available.

Otherwise, use any sheet material that you have in your equipment, anchoring it at the sides with turf blocks.

If none of these are available, make the shelter small and narrow enough to roof it over with long turf strips; use them in pairs so that they support each other. Whatever roofing method you use, try to give the roof a pitch of anything up to a 45-degree angle so that rain will run off it better.
Construction time: 1 to 2 hours.

Turf Shelter 2 Soft ground (but not wet) will provide the opportunity for a slight variation on the design of the above shelter. Build the wall up along the edge of the slit trench produced by the digging or cutting of the turf pieces. This not only saves effort by combining the digging and the building, but will also increase the height of your windbreak. If you do decide to adopt this method, ensure that the slope of the land and the shelter will drain rainwater away from the trench and not into it. Underground shelters are preferable in hot conditions, as they provide a cool space.
Construction time: 1 hour.

Parachute Tent A parachute, if you are lucky enough to have one, will be a valuable asset in building a shelter, as it can easily be made into a bell tent. First, the paracord rigging lines should to be removed; keep the cord, which is extremely valuable. Tie a long length of cord to the centre of the parachute. At the other end of the cord tie a heavy stone or log, and throw it over a suitable tree branch. Pull on the cord to raise the parachute to its full height, and then secure it to the trunk of the tree. Spread out the skirt of the parachute into a circle, and peg it into the ground. This should provide you with a shelter that is windproof and rainproof (as long as the material is not touched) although the fabric will not keep out very heavy rain.
Construction time: 20 minutes.

Tepee The parachute can be used to form the covering of a more traditional tepee. This will require a minimum of five thin poles which are at least 4 metres in length. Lay the poles side by side on the ground and lash them together at one end. Drape the parachute over the poles, passing the hole in the apex over the lashed-together pole tips and tying it securely to them. Get underneath the canopy and lift all the poles together until they are standing vertically. Splay the poles out in a circle until it becomes self-supporting.

Dangerous Shelter Sites

Always check shelter sites for possible dangers:

• Shelters too close to low-lying water may be in danger of sudden flooding.

• Coastal sites may be in danger from high tides or storms.

• An area of fallen trees in a forest may indicate shallow soil: in high wind falling trees could crush you.

• In mountainous areas, beware mud slides, rock falls and avalanches; check for visible evidence of previous slides.

• Outside Europe, do not camp too close to established animal trails.

Cordage is a central necessity for most survival tasks, from mending clothing and shoes to constructing packs, traps, tools and shelters.

Gather the surplus material at the skirt of the parachute and fold it up around the legs until you have formed a tepee. Cut a 'door' into the lee side of the tent in such a way that it can be fastened closed if necessary. Secure the parachute skirt with stones to prevent draughts.

Finding and Making Cord All survival kits should include a length of parachute cord; but many survival situations will also reveal several ways in which cordage can be produced. Parachutes contain at least 100 metres of excellent cord, from which the thin, inner strands can be extracted. Electric cable and control lines are also a valuable source of material for making lashings. Many military combat belts are made up of a series of strong cotton strips, and the material can be unravelled to make cordage.

Natural materials such as animal sinew and gut make ideal cordage. These are best dried and separated into the required thickness. Wetting them before use will allow for easy manipulation, while their hardening when dry will hold any knot firmly in place. The bark of some trees can be used, either in its natural state or split into stringy fibres.

Knots Knots and lashing are best kept simple, and require little or no explanation. If the survivor is unable to tie a secure knot then his chances of survival are fairly limited. It should also be remembered that any knot or lashing is only as strong as the material used in its construction. Knots and ropes are used in climbing, shelter construction, and a whole host of survival applications. A knot can join one or more ropes together, either permanently or for quick release depending on the requirement.

Utensils

Billy Can A 'billy can' is perhaps the most important utensil for the survivor – a container which can be used to collect water and plants, and also for cooking. Any metal container, such as a commercial-sized baked bean can, makes one of the best, with a wire handle attached for carrying.

Bamboo Bamboo has many uses, as jungle tribes have discovered over millennia. It can be used to make rafts, construct homes, build traps, and – because of its sectional nature – to make carrying, cooking and eating utensils.

Improvised Tools

1. A bone and a piece of metal will make a knife.

2. Bone will also make needles and buttons.

3. Wood is easy to carve to make a spoon.

4. Tree branches will provide a fork.

5. Chopsticks.

6. A branch will provide a useful cooking aid.

Know your Knots

The Reef Knot

The Clove Hitch

The Fisherman's Knot

The Figure Eight Bend

Birch Bark Containers Containers made from birch or cherry bark will not burn through when heated over a moderate fire, provided that you fill them with sufficient water. Cooking on a fire of glowing embers produces a better meal and extends the life of the bark container. Shoes can also be produced from such bark.

Eating Utensils If you have a penknife, you can construct a simple spoon from a flat piece of wood. Mugs can be made from a section of bamboo, a carved-out piece of wood, or a folded piece of birch bark. Many naturally occurring items can be fashioned into simple but adequate eating and drinking utensils with a little ingenuity and experimentation.

Tyres In survival situations brought about by vehicle accidents the survivor may well have access to tyres, which are a valuable resource. Tyre rubber can be cut up to make shoes and belts, and the reinforcing wire can be stripped out for traps and snares. Burning tyres create large amounts of black, acrid smoke which is excellent for signalling; for this reason they should normally be kept for use in rescue beacons rather than used for everyday fuel.

A tyre set in the middle of a three-pole frame makes a comfortable toilet seat; its value to morale should not be dismissed, particularly where survivors are suffering from digestive disorders.

Long Term Camp Routine

Long term camp routine implies that you will be permanently in one place for an unspecified length of time. To alleviate boredom and maintain a sense of personal discipline and hygiene certain routines need to be established, both for the individual and any group of survivors.

• In order to improve your existence you must become a scavenger and improviser. The world is full of rubbish discarded by thousands of travellers. From the inner forests of the Amazonian basin to the peaks of the Himalayas, and even in the vast wilderness of the polar regions, you will find the pollution of discarded man-made artefacts. To the survivor all this rubbish has a value.

• Long term camp sites can easily become contaminated with urine and faeces, and a strict routine should be organised as soon as your shelter and fire are finished. Dig toilet holes until a more permanent structure can be built. Collect your water upstream, and locate your washing point at least 50 metres downstream.

• Organize your day around the priorities of rescue, health and survival:

• Check your signal fires and markers, and always have your heliograph and signal flare with you at all times – Sod's Law dictates that you will be out of camp when the search aircraft flies over.

• Establish a disciplined pattern of working to prevent boredom and the consequent drop in morale. Get up early; make a warm drink; check your traps; collect firewood; make something useful.

In every extreme survival
situation, fire is essential.
Therefore the ability to light
a fire, even in difficult
conditions, is an invaluable
skill that needs to be learnt
and cultivated.

Practical and Morale Value

Fire has many obvious practical uses. Heat sustains wellbeing and life itself in cold or wet environments. Fire can be used to cook food, to dry clothes, to purify water and sterilize medical instruments, and to signal your rescuers. Waterborne diseases are one of the greatest dangers to survival (see Water section), but boiling will kill most harmful organisms. Hot drinks provide a vital source of body heat. Cooking food not only makes it more palatable, but also destroys many harmful organisms in animal products and neutralizes the toxins found in many plants.

Fire also plays an important psychological role in survival. Being able to build a fire proves to the survivor that he can control at least some elements of his situation and provide himself with the comfort of warmth and light. He will feel that he has achieved something positive by bringing back a hint of normality to his life.

To make a successful fire you need three elements: heat, oxygen, and fuel. If any element is missing your fire will not burn. However, before you even start to build any fire consider the following questions:

- Does the time you intend staying in your present location justify a fire?

- Do you really need a fire?

- Is there enough fuel nearby to sustain a fire?

- Are you in an area where fire could easily spread out of control?

Fire-starting Materials

Building a fire calls for an understanding of the dynamics involved. When any fuel is burned, part of the heat from that combustion will go on to ignite the next piece of fuel. The hotter a fire the better it will burn.

You do not need a great deal of heat for the initial ignition – a match is usually enough. However, because the first heat source is so small and lasts for only a short time, the material you apply it to must ignite very easily. This material we call tinder.

Feathered sticks make excellent kindling.

Tinder Whatever its source, tinder must fulfil certain criteria if it is to ignite readily. It must be bone dry and small in size, and must readily accept flame. Ideally the tinder should burn quickly, producing maximum heat. Included with tinder are certain combustible fuels; these may be in liquid, gel or solid form and are mostly manmade. Using ammunition or flares

Tinder Sources

Manmade:
• Petrol, paraffin or aviation fuel.

• Oil (needs heating first).

• Cooker gel or solid fuel blocks.

• Propellant explosive from ammunition (obtainable, with care, by prying bullet/shot out of cartridge case).

• Pyrotechnics – flares, etc.

• Tampons (check with any female survivors).

• Cotton wool (check any injured survivors for useful dressings).

• Lint from twine, canvas, bandages, etc.

• Scorched or charred cloth, especially linen.

• Charred rope.

• Some photographic film.

Natural:
• Decayed or powdered dry wood and pulverized bark.

• Catface (the resinous scab found on damaged evergreen trees).

• Coconut palm frond (the fabric-like material at the base needs to be sun-dried).

• Dried Arctic cotton grass or moss.

• Termite nest material.

• Birds', rats' or mice nests.

A successful fire is best started when it is shielded from the elements with fuel added gradually.

to start a fire can only be justified after carefully weighing the value of saving them for their original purpose. (See box for a list of tinder sources.)

Kindling Kindling consists of material larger in size than tinder but smaller than the main fuel to be used on the fire. Ideal candidates for kindling are small dry twigs, or shavings made from dry sticks, a process known as 'feathering'. Once your kindling takes hold, the fire should burn long enough to deal with small logs, i.e. the main fuel. Starter wood for fires needs to be dead and dry.

Fuel Your fuel should be graded and stacked ready before you start, with dry, dead material separated from green wood. A hot fire will be able to cope with green logs, as the flames will boil the sap away and dry the wood before it burns. However, green logs will not catch on a fire that is not well-established and hot.

Heaping the fuel on too quickly will kill a fire. Build your fire with care, adding more fuel only when the previous fuel is burning well. Do not stifle the fire by depriving it of the oxygen it needs – make sure it is well ventilated.

In principle, the harder the wood the longer it will burn. Try to use fuel that is close at hand, still

LIFESAVER

Carbon monoxide poisoning occurs when incomplete combustion of fuel takes place. In an unventilated enclosure it can quickly become lethal, especially when refined fuel such as petrol or aviation fuel is used. The following rules should be taken into account:

1 Always ensure good ventilation if using an oil burning stove.
2 Check any manufactured stove, and maintain its clean running.
3 Always turn off or extinguish any petrol or aviation type stove before going to sleep.

standing, and does not require chopping. If a log is too large, drag it into the fire and let it burn through the middle. Fuel taken from the forest floor will burn if stacked above ground for a few days, or placed around the edge of the fire to dry.

- Birch burns best.

- Both oak and ash burn well and give off good heat.

- Fruit trees such as apple and cherry give off scented smoke.

- Lighter woods such as larch and pine will spit sparks.

- For a concealed fire, burn elm.

Setting a Fire

The site for your fire must be chosen carefully, especially if you plan on building a shelter or if a strong wind is blowing. The heat should provide warmth for your shelter, but in such a way that the smoke does not envelope you (though if biting insects are a problem, a little smoke will help drive them off).

Constructing a windshield will prevent the wind from blowing out the first fledgling flames. It will also cut down the amount of fuel consumed, and reflect extra heat into your shelter.

The ground below your fire should be dry and clear of vegetation to stop the fire spreading.

If stones are available, build a circle around the fire once it is well alight. This reduces any danger of the fire setting your shelter or surroundings alight; it also defines the fire's size and fuel consumption.

If not maintained, such as overnight or while away hunting, a fire may well go out. Most fires can be relit by placing a small amount of tinder on top of the old embers and blowing. The earth below an old fire site will stay warm for many hours; this will help generate a new fire quickly.

Fire on Wet Ground To build a fire in swampy conditions the base must be raised above the water. In some cases this may mean building a platform of old logs or stones on which the fire

Heat Reflection

1 Fire reflector positioned to direct heat into shelter

2 Shelter sited in a position safely away from flames.

3 Smaller barrier to retain heat inside shelter

will rest. In extreme conditions a platform can be constructed several feet above the ground. One tribe who live in tree houses amid the jungle canopy of Malaysia cook with open fires using a base of stones and baked earth spread over the bamboo floor.

Fire in the Wind If the weather is extremely windy, a fire-shield will do little to stop the flames from getting out of control or being extinguished. In such conditions the only answer is to build your fire well below ground level, by either digging a trench or finding a natural ground hollow.

Ember Pit No matter what type of open fire you make, they are all difficult to cook on. Either they will burn the meat, or you will get burnt trying to rescue your supper. Metal cans become hot and the danger of scalding is inevitable. Rather than struggling with an open fire it is a good idea to make a small ember pit for cooking. This is simply a matter of cutting out a section of turf 20cm long by 10cm wide and 10cm deep (8ins x 4ins x 4ins). Once your fire is well established, use a stick to rake glowing embers into your pit. These will supply a manageable source of heat for cooking. As the embers die down or you require more heat, simply rake in more embers.

Sparks from a flint-and-steel were man s only portable fire-starting method for many centuries.

Lighting your Fire

The initial heat source for a fire can be produced in any number of ways. Matches or lighters provide the easiest option, but these will not last forever. Tinder can also be ignited by sparks from a flint-and-steel set, or from an electrical source such as a car battery. Heat from the sun can also be concentrated and focused by a magnifying glass or a parabolic reflector. Most heat sources are derived from commercially produced items, but if these are not available sufficient heat to light a fire can be generated by friction.

Matches Matches are the most convenient and obvious way of initiating a flame, and it is a matter of common sense that they should be carried as a matter of course on all outdoor trips. Ordinary matches do not work when damp, however, and can be quickly extinguished if unprotected from a strong wind. This fault can be remedied by dipping each match halfway into some molten wax. To protect the outside of the box, spray it with hair lacquer. Specially made survival matches are protected by a waterproof container, and when lit they will burn for up to 12 seconds in just about any weather conditions.

Lighters In any group of people several will probably be carrying cigarette lighters. These make an excellent survival aid, but must be used wisely and economically. Once the lighter fuel is exhausted do not just throw the lighter away – its flint will go on making sparks for a long time. A new device has also appeared on the survival market recently which converts a standard lighter into a mini-blowtorch.

Burning Glass Using a burning glass will require strong sunlight, but it can prove an effective way to light a fire given the right conditions. For the glass you could use a magnifying glass, or a lens from a camera, binoculars, spectacles or a compass. An ideal size would be 5cm (2ins) or more in diameter. Sunlight focused through the glass will ignite dry tinder, although you may need to fan it lightly as it smoulders.

Batteries If you have access to a large capacity battery from a vehicle, even if the vehicle has broken down or crashed, you may be able to start a fire by electrical means. Use a thin wire to connect the negative and positive terminals on the battery; this will short circuit the battery and cause the connecting wire to spark.

If very thin wire can be found, roll this into a ball and touch either end with both terminals; this will cause a flash bulb effect.

One Match, One Fire

You can save on matches and lighter fuel by lighting a candle with them immediately. This candle can then be used to provide a constant flame to ignite tinder, even when it is still a little damp. Like most naked flames, the candle should be protected from the wind by a shelter. Either dig a hole into the ground or build a small stone wall around it. Place the tinder over the flame, either by piling it on top of the shelter or building a small 'wigwam'. Once the tinder has ignited, remove the candle and if you no longer need it, blow out the flame and keep it for the next fire.

A burning glass will light tinder if the sun is strong enough.

Car Battery Method

❶ Use a thin strand of wire rolled into a ball around which you should place dry tinder.

❷ Connect two thicker insulated wires to the battery.

❸ Connect the insulated wires to the thin wire embedded in the tinder to create a spark.

Warning: If insulated wire is not available use two split sticks to hold the wires while making the connection.

Flint and Magnesium Fire Starter The specially manufactured flint is embedded into a small block of aluminium and magnesium metal which has a serrated steel striker attached. Shavings from the block can be scraped off and mixed in with any tinder. When the steel blade is struck sharply against the flint, sparks are produced which ignite the tinder. Magnesium burns in excess of 5,000° F, which is hot enough to ignite any tinder even when damp. In an emergency, scraping aluminium shavings from the frame of a crashed aircraft will produce very similar results.

Parabolic Reflector In hot, dry conditions with bright sunlight you can start a fire using a parabolic reflector (although in such conditions a fire may not be a necessity, and fuel may be scarce.)

LIFESAVER
Highly Inflammable Materials

Highly inflammable materials make very effective tinder, and if near a vehicle or aircraft always check to see if any are available. Sumps, fuel tanks, lubricants, alcohol, the propellant explosive from cartridges and pyrotechnics all burn.

- Handle them all with great care.
- Metal pots or implements should never be used when mixing chemicals.
- Many such substances will give off toxic gases when they burn.
- Remember that many chemicals which simply burn when loose are highly explosive when compressed or confined.

Illustrations in some survival books depicting a hand torch reflector being used in this way are highly improbable – your best bet is to use a vehicle headlamp. Place your tinder in the bulb housing; a very effective reflector can be achieved by removing the headlamp glass and replacing it in reverse, i.e. concave. Positioning a magnifying glass on the top of the headlamp and aiming it directly at the sun will cause any tinder to ignite instantly. Water can be boiled in a similar manner.

Chemicals Propellant explosives can be extracted from small arms ammunition or shotgun cartridges. It is best used by sprinkling it over dry tinder and applying a spark (beware – even small concentrations of such chemicals are potentially dangerous). Simple gunpowder – 'black powder' – is not found in modern cartridges; but it is mixed from equal amounts of potassium nitrate, sulphur and charcoal. Another mixture with a high output of heat is sugar and sodium chlorate (found in some commercial weedkillers) mixed in equal parts. This will be hot enough to light a fire even from damp tinder.

Fire Paste Fire paste is highly volatile and should be kept for emergency fire-lighting only (see Arctic Survival section). It is basically any combustible material that is held in a suitable base: aviation fuel mixed with soap is one example. A small spark will normally ignite the paste, which will then burn for several minutes. As with any combustible material, the paste should be kept in an airtight container when not in use.

In a dire emergency the paste can be burnt purely as a fuel.

Fire Torch Cane has been used to make torches since prehistoric times. One end is split and separated in order to hold some form of burning material. Where the wind is not troublesome this can even be a candle. Birch bark rolled, split and dried also makes a good torch.

A cane and birch torch.

Carrying Fire

One sure method of making a quick fire especially in the cold and wet is to carry embers from your previous fire. Many early hunters transported fire around in a cow or buffalo horn.

This method can still be used simply using a perforated beer or coke can as a fire carrier. The skill remains in packing the embers from last night's fire onto a bed of dry, slow-burning material, and covering them with the same. The secret lies in the ability to maintain the correct amount of oxygen being fed to the embers. If they are wrapped too tightly, they will be starved of air, if too loose there is a danger that the embers will ignite the surrounding material.

Fire from Friction

Creating fire from friction may be the only method left to a survivor, particularly when his consumable means of fire-making, such as matches, have run out. Many primitive peoples around the world still light their fires by friction; it is presumably the oldest method of creating a flame, and certainly dates back to our prehistoric ancestors. Although methods vary from continent to continent, the following covers the basic principles of fire by friction.

Fire Plough The fire plough method involves rapidly rubbing a hardwood shaft against a softwood base. Under ideal conditions both woods should be seasoned so that the moisture content is minimal. In an emergency this can be achieved by sun-drying green wood, although it will take several days.

The baseboard should measure around 30cm by 10cm (12ins by 4ins) and have a straight central channel cut down the entire length of one side. One end of the shaft should be rounded to fit into this groove, and ground up and down the baseboard channel – adding a little sand will speed up this process. Once both the tip of the shaft and the channel have become blackened and smoke can be seen rising, the fire plough is ready for use. Kneel and place the baseboard against the left thigh. Grip the shaft with both hands and make a sharp, stabbing, ploughing action. As you build up speed small particles of wood fibres will fall to the ground. Place a small amount of dry tinder at the base of the channel ready to catch these. Once the tinder is smouldering, blow on it until you have fire.

The fire pump or piston, an ingenious invention, thought to have originated in the Orient.

Fire Piston or Pump To the best of my knowledge the fire piston evolved in the Far East. It might have been invented by the Chinese or possibly the Japanese, who until recently commonly used brass cylinders of a similar type for lighting cigarettes.

The fire pump requires a body into which a 12cm (4.75in) long chamber has been reamed, similar to the barrel of a gun. A piston, with a handle to assist pressure, is inserted into the chamber. The end of the piston is cup-shaped, and into this a small amount of dry tinder is placed. The piston is then thrust rapidly into the chamber forcing the air molecules to compress, generating enough heat to convert the tinder into glowing embers.

The walls of the 'barrel' have to be straight, smooth and lightly greased. To assure an airtight fit, thread should be carefully wrapped around the piston about 2cm above the tinder cup, and this too can be lightly greased. The tinder needs to be bone dry and extremely light. The downy vest from between the layers of a banana palm stem, dried in the sunlight, is used locally in the Far East; however, during experiments I found that dried mushroom, cotton wool and even charcoal will ignite in a well-made fire pump. Making my own fire piston brought me to the conclusion that it needs to be a precision-made device. That said, a good one would last almost indefinitely.

Experience and precision play a large part in getting the fire piston to work. Ram the piston all the way down the chamber with a half-blow, half-push motion, then withdraw immediately. Keep the withdrawn piston upright so that the glowing embers don't fall out.

Bow & Drill The basis of this classic method is a flat dry board of powdery wood and a hardwood stick. The principle is to make a hole in the flat board into which the hardwood stick – i.e. the drill – will fit neatly. The baseboard can be any length, but 30cm by 10cm by a minimum of 2cm thick is ideal. Cut a V-shaped notch about 2cm wide on one edge.

The drill should be made from a length of medium-hard wood such as elm, willow, cedar, cypress, cottonwood or balsam fir. Make sure that the chosen piece is sound and dry, and that you are able to cut a straight length from it 20-25cm long and 2cm thick. Sharpen one end of the drill to a 45 degree point and the other end to a 60 degree point.

The baseboard should be placed on the ground and held in place by the toe of your boot. Place a small ball of tinder directly under the notch cut in the baseboard, dropping a little into the notch

Using a Fire Drill

• The ideal wood for the board is old deadfall, dried-out and powdery.

• The ideal drill is a sound, dry length of hardwood.

• Use your best available tinder.

• Settle yourself comfortably, so you can drill for hours if necessary.

• Don't give up – you will need hours of patience.

• Have extra tinder handy to add when you see smoke.

• Have fine, dry kindling handy to add as soon as you have blown the sparks in your tinder into flame.

• Shelter and nurture your burning kindling until you can add small, dry fuel.

itself. The best tinder is dried grass mixed with small strips of cedar or birch bark. Fit the sharper end of the drill into the notch of the baseboard, and prepare to rotate it backwards and forwards. This can be done by rubbing the drill between your palms, but using a bow is better.

Make a small bow about 60cm-70cm long, and loosely string it with a length of cord or leather thong. Twist a loop in the bow-string and slip it over the drill. Pushing the bow back and forth will rotate the drill in the base-board notch. Extra pressure can be placed on the drill by using some form of cup over the upper end to hold it in place; in my experience a near-perfect expedient is a small glass jar, as used to hold fish paste.

Using a fire drill. It may take hours of work before the drill starts to smoke.

Do not expect to make a fire instantly; the drill will need to 'bed' itself into the baseboard, and this can only be achieved after hours of constant drilling.

An indication that you are close to producing hot embers will come when the drill becomes charred and smoke can be seen   rising from the notch. Add a little tinder to the notch, and work the drill vigorously. Embers from the notch should fall into the tinder below. Carefully move the block away and blow gently on the pile until the tinder ignites. As with any survival skill, practice makes perfect.

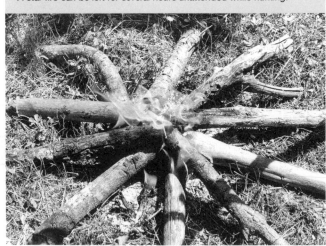

A star fire can be left for several hours unattended while hunting.

Types of Fire

Once you have a fire, you need to make sure that it is suitable for your needs. If you are alone you will only need a small fire for warmth. Small fires need less fuel to keep them going, and can be controlled more easily.

If it is snowing or raining – and if you have the means – you should consider taking your fire inside your shelter; and the best way to do this is to improvise a stove. You can also build a fire that will cook your food while you are hunting, and warm your bed on a cold night.

Star Fire This is a simple and easily controlled fire. Once the fire is established, place logs so that they can be fed inwards, increasing the flames. If less heat is required the logs can be pulled outwards. You can leave this fire for several hours while you go hunting. The flames will eventually die down, leaving the hot embers in the middle; these can be protected from wet weather by placing a large stone over the inward ends of the logs. When you return, carefully remove the warm stone and use it as a seat. To rekindle the fire simply push the logs closer together and gently fan or blow on the embers.

Lumberman's Fire A lumberman's fire is built using two long logs – the larger branches from fallen trees are ideal. The purpose is to build a normal fire between the logs until the fire has reached the point where the logs themselves will burn. If the timing is right you should be able to cook your food on the small fire in between before rolling the logs together. You will then be able to stretch out for the night along the length of the burning logs, and have a good sleep. Separating the logs in the morning and adding a few twigs will

A pyramid fire will provide good heat and a bright flame for signalling.

Hot bed

One way to reflect the heat from your fire is to stack large stones around the back of the fire. The advantage of this method is that the hot stones can then be taken into your shelter at night and carefully placed beneath your bed space. There they will radiate heat throughout the night hours.

Spontaneous Combustion

A survivor will seldom be carrying the right chemicals to produce spontaneous combustion. If, however, the right substances are available – e.g. antifreeze from a vehicle radiator, potassium permanganate from the medical kit – you can use them to start a fire.

Antifreeze will contain enough glycerine to start a chemical reaction with potassium permanganate crystals. This reaction involves rapid oxidization, generating great heat.

❶ Take a teaspoonful of potassium permanganate crystals and place them on a sheet of paper, cloth or some other inflammable material.

❷ Add 2 or 3 drops of antifreeze, and roll the sheet up tightly – this is vital in order to concentrate the heat in one spot, thereby raising the temperature to flashpoint (for paper this is 451°F).

❸ After a short delay – perhaps 1 minute – the mixture should ignite and set fire to the tinder.

An improvised tin stove.

quickly rekindle the fire for breakfast.

Pyramid Fire Building a pyramid fire is simply a matter of placing logs in a pattern to create a pyramid-shaped stack. Smaller and drier twigs and sticks can be placed inside the fire or threaded between the layers.

This type of fire, once lit, will burn quickly and provide plenty of heat. It can also form the basis of a signal fire (see Signalling).

Improvised Stove
Constructing a stove from any available metal drum is a vast improvement on a simple open

fire. A stove will save fuel, as it is 50% more economical than an open fire. With care, it can be used inside a shelter, with the outer metal radiating enough heat to dry wet clothing while the stove provides light. If not too large it can be carried with you, complete with hot or burning embers.

Benghazi Stove If liquid fuel is available then a simple stove can be constructed by simply filling a large can half full of sand. The fuel is added until the sand is completely saturated. It is best to burn a small amount of tinder on top of the sand; this preheats the fuel and ignites the sandy surface, which provides a good slow-burning flame. Peat or fine gravel can be used if sand is not available. A fuel candle can be produced in the same way by using a smaller can and a strip of old cloth or rope.

Steps to Remember

1 Choose a suitable site and prepare it for the fire.

2 Gather an ample supply of fuel, grade it into categories and stack it.

3 Prepare your tinder.

4 Light the fire with small amounts of your driest fuel, and nurse it until it is burning hotly.

5 Add new material to it slowly – you do not want to smother it.

6 Check ventilation if there is any risk of carbon monoxide poisoning.

Start your pyramid fire quickly by building a small stack of feathered sticks and dry twigs in the centre.

Fire Management

• Don't make your fire so large that you can't get near it to put a pot on.

• It is safer and better to cook using only the embers.

• If you have the means to make one, an improvised stove is more economical of fuel than an open fire, and more versatile in use.

• Keep plenty of fuel handy, and near enough to the fire to dry out before use.

• Stop your fire spreading: it's dangerous, and wasteful. Beyond a certain size you get no additional benefit from a larger blaze – and your energy expended in gathering fuel is ultimately wasted in the sky above your fire.

• If you stay in the same place for any period of time, use the same spot for your fire.

• Keep drying clothes far enough away not to fall into the fire.

Next to air, water plays the most vital part in daily survival. The human body, which consists of roughly 90% water, cannot survive without water longer than three days in a hot climate and 12 days in a cold one.

In a temperate climate, carrying out a normal level of activity, the body requires a daily fluid intake of 2.5 litres (roughly 4.5 pints). This requirement fluctuates according to the humidity, air temperature and amount of physical activity undertaken. To keep the body efficient and to have a chance of survival, the minimum daily water requirements must be met. It is not only the quantity of water that is important, but also the quality. Contaminated or impure water will do the survivor more harm than good, increasing both fluid loss and the risk of serious disease.

Water Loss

Water is continually lost through the normal bodily functions of urination, excretion, breathing and sweating. The amount of water lost through sweating is notably increased when in hot conditions or during physical activity. This water must be replaced. If, however, your water supply is minimal, the priority is to conserve as much water in the body as is possible (see box).

Drinkable Water Sources

Even if you practice all possible precautions, without a good supply of potable water they will only prolong your survival by a few days. It is imperative to locate or extract water from any source available while being equally cautious about filtration and purification. Waterborne diseases and parasites pose a great health risk to the survivor, but this risk needs to be balanced against that of dying of thirst

Rain, streams and rivers provide the majority of the world's drinkable water, but it is not always easy to find.

Animals and insects will give some indication of water being present: watch grazing animals in the early dawn or at sundown, as this is when they will make their way to water. If surface water cannot be found, try looking in valley bottoms for signs of vegetation, and start digging. Water can sometimes be found high up in the mountains where storm water and mist have collected in natural cisterns. If neither surface nor sub-surface water can be located, you can acquire it from a host of sources.

Collecting water in a polythene bag placed over foliage.

Plant Sources Water is collected by a variety of plants; it is contained in living vines and can be extracted from cacti.

Covering foliage with a clear polythene bag is one easy way of gathering moisture – this literally pumps the water from the ground for you. Vegetation of all kinds takes water from the soil and distributes it to

LIFESAVER
Dangerous Water

Watching animals may lead you to water; but beware of drinking directly from stagnant pools where animals drink, as they transfer a variety of harmful parasites into the water through infected urine or faeces.

Leptospirosis, bilharzia, and dysentery are just a few diseases which can be caused by drinking contaminated water.

- **Animal bones in the vicinity of stagnant water may mean that the water is poisonous.**
- **Always sterilize or if possible distil water from ponds.**
- **Approach any isolated watering hole with caution, as it will be visited by a large number of animal species – some of which have large teeth and are permanently hungry.**

An improvised water filter

the leaves, where it is released as part of the respiration process. Find a suitable green plant and place the bag over the top of a piece of healthy green foliage, tying the neck around the base of the plant. Next to the plant, dig out a small hollow and press the plastic into it to form a collection point for the condensing moisture.

In a similar way the moisture contained in plant stems and leaves can be extracted. In springtime tapping into certain trees, such as the birch, will produce a drinkable sap. Make a hole in the tree one metre above ground level; the hole should be about 5cm (2ins) deep and slanting slightly upwards. Tap a peg into the hole and place your container on the ground below. You should collect 2 litres (3.5 pints) over a 24-hour period. Boil the sap to make it more palatable and prevent it going off. In a survival situation you might try other types of tree; but be aware that milky or coloured saps or juices may be poisonous.

Dew Large droplets of early morning dew can be found on most vegetation, especially grass. This is particularly helpful for those

A drinking straw allows you to drink from water extraction or condensation devices whose product may not be easy to pour out into a container.

A water filter pump.

A filter hole.

survivors who are injured and cannot move far. The droplets can be mopped up by gently laying a clean cloth over the wet grass, and wringing it out. Several pints can be collected in less than an hour, and the water is pure enough to drink without sterilization.

Filtering Filtering will remove mud particles, leaves and small waterborne creatures. This can be done using a clean sock, a shirtsleeve (or women's tights in the case of female survivors), a plastic bottle or a section of bamboo. Fill the makeshift filter with a layer of fresh grass or moss; then add either sun-dried sand or charcoal from an old fire. Allow contaminated water to filter through and run out the bottom end. Don't worry about the water being discoloured, especially if you are filtering with charcoal or are using peat water; this will do no harm.

Filter Hole A filter hole can be made in any form of waterlogged terrain such as a swamp, bog or marsh.

Clear the vegetation and dig a hole above the water line, measuring approximately 30cm (12ins) in diameter and 30cm deep. The water which seeps into the hole may be dark in colour; this of itself is of no consequence, but the water will need boiling to kill off the micro-bacteria and viruses. If you do not have the means to dig, simply remove a large stone or log and let the well underneath it fill up.

Sterilization and Distillation

Once you have filtered your water the next stage is to sterilize it. Sterilization can be achieved by boiling water vigorously for at least ten minutes. Make sure that the heat is distributed evenly – keep your water on a rolling boil.

Contained water, urine and seawater can all be made drinkable by distillation. This is a process whereby the contaminated water is

Sterilizing Water

• Drinking bad water causes weakening sickness, and is more dangerous than thirst.

• Filter water first, using moss and charcoal.

• Kill off micro-bacteria and viruses by adding chlorine-based purification tablets.

• If you have no purification tablets, use potassium permanganate crystals.

• If you have no chemical agents, then boil water hard for 10 minutes minimum.

converted to steam by boiling; the resulting steam is condensed and converted back into good drinking water. The process can be carried out with or without the aid of a fire, although some form of heat is required.

Another simple precaution is chemical sterilization, e.g. using chlorine-based purification tablets, potassium permanganate (see Survival Medical Pack), or iodine. Be sure to follow the instructions for use carefully.

Chemical sterilization tends to leave an unpleasant taste and odour in the water, and both the iodine and potassium will stain the water pink. Adding small pieces of charcoal to the water an hour before you want to drink it can rectify this.

Carrying Water

The survivalist should carry a supply of water even when travelling through an area where it is abundant. There is always the possibility that a lone survivor will fall or otherwise injure himself and be unable to walk. Any available container can be used, but those with a screw cap are best. Bottles, waterproof cloth, condoms, animal intestine and bamboo can all be fashioned into makeshift water carriers.

Salt

Salt is next in importance to water, as it helps to regulate the fluid balance in the body. Without an adequate supply you will succumb to muscular cramps, heat exhaustion and heatstroke.

Conserving Body Fluid

• Dehydration kills quickly, but drinking contaminated water kills quicker and is more painful.

• Examine all possible water sources available to you.

• Evaluate water supplies, and discipline their use.

• Exposed skin should be covered, as this will reduce water loss.

• Cool your body to reduce your sweating. Fan yourself; in a sea survival situation, wet clothes with seawater.

• Minimize movement on hot days; work or travel by night; avoid unnecessary exertion.

• Close the mouth and breathe through the nose.

• Avoid eating where possible.

• Drink when the day is at its coolest. Take small sips.

• Alcohol consumption and smoking will cause further dehydration.

Heavy duty non-lubricated condoms will hold up to 1.5 litres of water supported in a sock or shirt sleeve.

The average human body requires about 10gm (0.35 oz) of salt daily to replace that lost in normal sweating. When the body is deficient in salt, the first signs are sudden weakness, muscle cramps, dizziness, nausea and a hot, dry feeling all over the body.

If these symptoms appear, rest and a pinch of salt in a mug of water are the quickest and easiest treatment.

Salt deficiency is common in arid or tropical jungle conditions, so in these environments it makes sense to ensure that you add a small amount of salt to your drinks. It would also be a wise precaution to add some salt tablets to your personal survival kit.

Food is not an immediate factor in survival. The average adult can go 14 days without food before any serious effects start to impair physical ability, and death from starvation takes well over a month.

That said, all survivors should be on the look-out for food from day one; if it grows, walks, crawls, swims or flies it is probably edible.

Animals and plants form the two sources of food available from the wild. Animals provide food rich in energy, protein and many nutrients, but the survivor will usually have to expend much time, effort and energy to catch and prepare them. The amount and type of food you will be able to eat will also depend upon your water supply.

If it is scarce, you must avoid any dry, starchy food or salty meat, since these will make you thirsty. Instead eat foods that are high in carbohydrates, such as wild plants.

Plant Food

Compared to the problems of catching animals, plant food is easy to gather and is usually available in one form or another every-where except in areas of the most extreme climatic conditions. The plant species will determine its richness in vitamins and minerals. Although some plants are very low in food value, they can still be sustaining.

In a long-term survival situation plant food on its own will not provide a fully balanced diet, and you may have to eat more than normal to fulfil your body's requirements. However, in times of need plants are a valuable resource and will keep you from starving.

Some knowledge of edible plants is required, as over half of all plant species are inedible or poisonous. Of those that are edible, only certain parts of the plant may be palatable. Whether you die of starvation or take the chance of eating a poisonous plant will be a personal decision at the time. If you choose the latter, you should at least take the precaution of doing an edibility test (see overleaf). Although not infallible this does give some indication of the human body's reaction to the plant.

Tap Roots

The most natural-seeming parts of a plant to eat are the young leaves and shoots. However, valuable carbohydrate can be obtained by cleaning and cooking the fleshy tap root or rhizome of some plants, notably dandelion, bracken, goat's beard, flowering rush, arrowhead and many more.

Some edible plants contain elements that are dangerous to health if they build up in the body. Therefore be wary of eating too much of the same plant, especially over long periods. A varied vegetable diet will not only be tastier but will also provide much more balanced nutrition.

The plants mentioned below are intended only as a guide. They represent only a small representative fraction of the plants which have uses as either food or medicine or both. It is recommended that you read about the plants that are native to the area where you intend to travel – learn to recognize them and know their properties, in order to keep yourself and others safe.

LIFESAVER
THE EDIBILITY TEST

The edibility test is a time-consuming and thorough process. Although it may appear to be over-cautious, remember that your very survival is at stake. Plant poisons may take time before they have any effect on the body; also, plants may affect people in different ways. Make sure that you carry out plant testing before your food stocks are depleted, not after.

• A plant's identity must be 100% established. If for any reason you are at all unsure whether it is edible or not, follow the simple steps below.

• Be scientific and thorough in your testing. Test only one plant and one person at a time, so that any effects can be well monitored.

• The plant edibility test will **NOT work for fungi**.

• Avoid collecting plants from any area which may have been contaminated, and those with milky saps (except for dandelion, goat's beard and coconut).

• Wash any plant material thoroughly before cooking, and remove any diseased or damaged parts.

• Not all the parts of any one plant may be edible. Separate the root, stem, leaves and any fruit. Treat each part individually with the same test.

• Only test plants which are plentiful in your environment. There is no point in subjecting your body to possible poisoning if there is only a handful of the plant available.

The Test

❶ **First test the plant for any contact poisons. Crush a leaf and rub a little of the sap onto the sensitive skin of the inner wrist. If after 15 minutes no itching, blistering or burning has occurred, continue.**

❷ **Take a small portion of crushed plant and place it in your mouth between your gum and lower lip. Leave it for 5 minutes, testing for any unpleasant reactions.**

❸ **If there are none, chew the plant; note whether it exhibits any disagreeable properties such as burning, extreme bitterness, or a soapy taste.**

❹ **If it still gives no reason for suspicion, swallow down the juice but spit out the pulp.
Allow 8 hours to pass to see if it has any adverse effects on the body, such as sickness, dizziness, sleepiness, stomach aches or cramps.**

❺ If none of these symptoms occur, eat a slightly larger amount, e.g. a teaspoonful, and wait for another 8 hours.

❻ If there are still no negative results, eat a handful of the plant and wait for a further 24 hours.

❼ If after this period the plant has given you no ill effects, you can assume that it is safe and can be eaten in greater quantities.

Use all your senses

• As well as the taste test described, use your eyes; brightly coloured plants may be poisonous.

• Watch to see if other animals eat the plant.

• Smell may also provide you with clues to a plant's safety – be wary of plants emitting pungent odours.

Some Edible Plants

Sorrel (Rumex acetosa) A perennial plant that is most usually found on grassland and also on waste ground.

It has an erect stem crowned with long flower bracts, the flowers themselves concentrated in small pink clusters. The leaves are long and taper to a point, with their lower lobes pointing downwards to the base. High in vitamin C, the young leaves, buds and shoot tips can be eaten in salads, soups or stews. Be aware that this plant also contains high levels of oxalic acid, a poison that can build up in the body and cause organ damage. Therefore be careful not to eat too much of this plant at one time, and avoid eating it frequently.

Sorrel

Dandelion (Taraxacum officinale)

Distribution: Northern Temperate regions up to 2000m (6,500ft).

Habitat: Meadows, pastures, roadsides, waste ground.

Perennial. Stems, up to 30cm (12ins) long and containing a milky latex, grow from a long, fleshy tap root.

Leaves are dark green and deeply toothed; at the plant's base they form a rosette. The solitary flowers appear from March to August and are bright yellow in colour.

Availability: Leaves and roots can be used all year round.

Edibility: The young leaves can be eaten raw in a salad, although they do have a very bitter taste; this can be remedied by soaking the leaves in cold water for a couple of hours. Older leaves can also be eaten but will need to have the tough central vein removed first; they will be more palatable if boiled. The newest shoots, picked before the stems develop, can be boiled and used like Brussels sprouts. The tap roots, once cleaned, can be boiled as you would a root vegetable; the taste is very pleasant. The roots can also provide a good substitute for coffee, if dried and crushed.

Medicinal: The leaves have a mild diuretic effect. The juice from the root, usually extracted by boiling, makes a good tonic for the liver and the digestion. The leaves are rich in vitamins A and C and are also a good source of iron and potassium.

Greater Plantain (Plantago major)

Distribution: Northern Temperate regions up to 600m (2,000ft).

Habitat: Grassland, riverbanks, hedges, roadsides. The greater plantain has large oval leaves which form a loose rosette at the base of the plant. The leaves are dark green and are rarely toothed. The smooth stem always rises above the leaves to a height of about 20-45cm (7-18ins). The very small flowers, brownish in colour, are closely packed together on a cylindrical spike. The ribwort plantain has narrow, pointed leaves rising out of a basal rosette. The stem is deeply grooved and the flower spike is not as long as that of the greater plantain.

Availability: All year round.

Edibility: The leaves of both plants can be eaten, although they are much more palatable when young, when they can even be eaten raw. Older leaves need to have their fibrous ribs removed and should then be boiled, as you would for any greens. They are rather bitter and are generally best added to stews.

Medicinal: An infusion of either plant will soothe bronchial coughs. The juice expressed from the plant will help wounds to heal.

Stinging Nettle (Urtica diotica)

Distribution: Common throughout Temperate regions.

Habitat: Woods, hedges, waste ground, sheltered grassy places. A perennial plant that grows up to a height of 120cm (46ins). The stems bear heart-shaped, toothed leaves which are covered in small stinging hairs. The lesser nettle (urtica urens) is much smaller and is an annual.

Availability: Best eaten in March/April when shoots are young.

Edibility: Young nettle shoots make a good vegetable, but they need to be boiled first as this removes the stinging properties of the juice. They make a very tasty, nutritious soup, and can be added to stews.

Medicinal: Freshly pressed nettle juice is a good tonic and helps the digestion. A tea made from nettles will help to ease rheumatism, and, if left to cool and applied externally, can soothe burns, sunburn, insect bites and minor skin irritations. Young nettle shoots are rich in vitamin C, although much of this vitamin will be lost in the cooking process. Nettles are also rich in iron and other minerals. Older leaves should be avoided if possible, as they are full of uric acid crystals which can cause kidney damage. If you must eat them, boil very thoroughly first.

Other uses: The fibres from older nettles have been used in the past to make yarn for clothing and twine.

Bracken (Pteridium Aquilinum)

Distribution: Throughout the world, except the extreme south and north.

Habitat: Heaths, moors, woods. A perennial which can grow up to 8ft (2.4m) in the right conditions, but is usually only about 2-3ft (0.6-0.9m) in height. The stem is erect and tree-like, with a velvety feel to it at the base. It carries large pinnate fronds, usually three on each stem. The young fronds are coiled inwards but soon unfold, and can be seen to have three prongs. The rootstock or rhizome is long, thick and succulent, and creeps horizontally beneath the soil. Be careful not to confuse this plant with the male fern which can be found growing alongside bracken. The male fern tends to have only one frond.

Bracken

Plant Infusions

A 'tea' or infusion made from many naturally occuring plants will have mild but beneficial medicinal properties.

- **Silverweed**
- **Coltsfoot**
- **Greater Plantain**
- **Ribwort Plantain**
- **Stinging Nettle**
- **Daisy**
- **Blackberry**
- **Hawthorn**
- **Clover**

Availability: All year round.
Edibility: The young fronds can be cooked as vegetables, like asparagus, although you will need to scrape the hairs off first. They also need to be boiled for about 30 minutes as they tend to be very bitter otherwise. The starchy rhizome can be cleaned and roasted; the inner portion can then be eaten.
Medicinal: None, although the rhizome's astringent qualities may make it useful for healing wounds.
Other uses: Bracken makes good bedding material, and also can be used to thatch the roof of a shelter. When burnt, bracken ash contains high proportions of potash. When the ash is mixed with a little water or fat it can be used as a soap substitute.

Daisy (Bellis perennis)

Distribution: Common throughout Temperate regions.
Habitat: Grasslands and meadows. Small perennial plant. Leaves are arranged in a basal rosette; erect stems produce white, many-petalled flowers from early summer to late autumn.
Availability: Spring and summer.

Daisy

Edibility: The leaves from the basal rosette can be added to salads raw or added to soups, although they have quite an acrid, pungent taste. Young flower buds can be treated in the same way.
Medicinal: Made as a tea, an infusion of daisies will help combat catarrh, rheumatism, arthritis, liver and kidney problems, and diarrhoea. Also a good blood purifier.

Bramble, Blackberry (Rubus fruticosus)

Distribution: Northern Temperate regions below 450m (1,500ft).
Habitat: Woods, heath, scrub, wasteland, hedges. A perennial decid-uous shrub with long, arching, thorny stems forming intertwining

Bramble

bushes. The leaves are mid green, pinnate, with five to seven toothed leaflets. The flowers are pale pink and may be seen on the bush at the same times as the fruits. When ripe the latter are black in colour and consist of many segments.
Availability: Spring to autumn.
Edibility: The ripe berries are the obvious food of the bramble and can be eaten raw or in salads. A refreshing drink can also be made from them. Blackberry leaves also make an excellent tea. For this, the leaves must either be very fresh, or will need to be slowly dried and crushed.
Medicinal: The leaves of the blackberry are very astringent, so a tea made from them is effective in treating diarrhoea and gum problems. High in vitamin C.

Hawthorn (May) (Crataegus monogyna)

Distribution: Europe, North Africa, Western Asia.

Habitat: Woods, hedges, scrubland. Small tree or shrub which can reach a height of 9m (30ft). It has light-coloured bark and is covered in thin thorns. In spring it produces plentiful white blossom, which from July to October bear small red fruit, 1cm (0.4in) in diameter with a small stone in the centre.

Availability: Spring, autumn.

Edibility: The young buds can be eaten raw, and young leaves may be added to stews. The fruit can also be eaten, and – contrary to popular belief – are not bitter.

Medicinal: A tea made from the flowers or fruits will soothe sore throats, and help to ease diarrhoea.

Other uses: Hawthorn is an extremely hard wood and makes one of the best fuels, as it burns very hot.

Preparation

All plants and leaves should be washed in fresh water before consumption. While some of them can be eaten raw, it is generally safer to cook all food. Add plants and berries to other dishes, such as stews and soups. Not only will the addition enhance the taste of the food, but it will also add to the general nutritional values of your cooking.

Roots and tubers can be boiled, but they are much better baked or roasted. Wash or scrape first.

Hawthorn

Rowan (Sorbus aucuparia)

Distribution: Throughout the Temperate regions.

Habitat: Mountains, hillsides, hedgerows and woodland. This delicate-looking deciduous tree can also be found in places that have been, or still are, inhabited by humans It grows up to 20m (65ft) high, with pinnate leaves and a smooth, grey bark.

Availability: White flowers appear in May to June, and are followed by bunches of red berry-like fruits in July to September.

Edibility: The fruits are edible; although not poisonous raw, they are extremely bitter. To counteract this the berries should be briefly boiled and then the water discarded.

Medicinal: The fruits contain high proportions of vitamin C. An infusion of the dried flowers and fruit can help to combat constipation, and rheumatic pains. The juice of the fresh fruit has the same effect.

Goat's Beard (Tragopogon pratensis)

Distribution: Throughout the Temperate regions.

Habitat: Grassland and waste ground. A dandelion-like annual or perennial plant, it has a tall stem containing a white sap. The leaves, which grow up the stem, start by semi-clasping the stem and then tapering to a sharp point. Both stem and leaves have distinctive white veins. The flower heads are large and solitary, having yellow petals which close at mid-day.

Edibility: Before flowering, the young plant and buds can be eaten like asparagus. Most of the young plant, including the root, can also be chopped up for use in salads, soups or stews. Once the plant is more mature the root can still be used, although it should be blanched, peeled and boiled first.

Wild Rose (Rosa canina)
Distribution: Throughout the Temperate regions.
Habitat: Hedges, woodland and scrub. Deciduous in nature, the green or brown stems have an arching habit and are covered in many hooked thorns. The leaves are pinnate. The pale pink flowers are usually solitary and have no scent. The fruit, appearing in autumn, is red, shiny and smooth, and contains many seeds.
Edibility: The fruits or hips can be boiled up to make a syrup, or added to soups. However, before they are used the seeds and hairs must be removed, as these are irritants.
Medicinal: Rose hips are full of vitamin C, and provide a very useful tonic against exhaustion and colds. For this, boil the finely chopped fruit for ten minutes. This drink is also effective against constipation.

Wild Rose

Clovers (Trifolium pratense and Trifolium repens)
Distribution: Throughout the Temperate regions.
Habitat: Both red and white clovers can be found commonly on grassland. They are perennial plants with distinctive three-lobed leaves. The white clover differs from the red not only by the colour of its flowers but also by the fact that it possesses a long, creeping rootstock, the means by which it spreads. The flowers of the white clover are scented.
Edibility: The most edible part of both types of the clover plant is the leaves, before the plant flowers. They can either be cooked on their own, like spinach, or they can be added to soups, stews, sauces and salads. The flowers can be dried and used as a tea substitute.

Crab Apples (Malus sylvestris)
Distribution: Throughout the Temperate regions.
Habitat: Woods, hedges and scrubland. The wild apple, like cultivated varieties, is deciduous. The height can range from a scrubby bush to a tree 11m (36ft) tall. The bark is greyish brown and rough, the leaves oval in shape. White-pink flowers appear in spring and are arranged in clusters on the end of twigs. The fruits which follow are round, greenish-yellow, and usually over 2cm (0.8in) in diameter.
Edibility: Wild apples are extremely acidic and sour to the taste. They are best cooked with other fruits if a bad case of diarrhoea is to be avoided.

Hazel (Corylus avellana)
Distribution: Throughout the Temperate regions.
Habitat: Woods and hedges. The hazel does not usually grow very tall, and often appears more like a shrub than a tree. The bark is smooth and red-brown in colour, and the leaves are almost round in shape. The most visible flowers are the male

catkins which appear in spring; they are followed in autumn by the familiar fruit, the hazel nuts.

Edibility: The nut is pleasant to eat on its own and also highly nutritious, being rich in oils and vitamins. The oil can also be crushed out of the nut to provide a cooking oil.

Hazel

Coltsfoot (Tussilago farfara)
Distribution: Throughout the Temperate regions.

Habitat: Waste ground, banks, scree and dunes. The remarkable feature of this perennial plant is that the yellow flowers and their purple stems appear in March/April, ahead of the leaves which come forth in May. The leaves are large, polygonal in shape and have a whitish look to their underside.

Edibility: The young leaves are edible, either eaten raw in a salad or cooked in soups and vegetable dishes. The same applies to the young shoots and flowers. Coltsfoot has a rather aromatic flavour which is quite pleasant once one has got used to it.

Coltsfoot

Medicinal: An infusion of coltsfoot leaves, either fresh or dried, will help to soothe coughs and will calm the stomach if digestive problems occur. Small cuts and wounds can also be helped to heal by placing a bruised coltsfoot leaf on them.

Water Chestnut (Trapa natans)
Distribution: Widespread in Eurasia.

Habitat: Free-floating plant found in quiet water. It has arrow-shaped leaves which float on the surface in a rosette, and also possesses sub-aquatic leaves which are long and feathery. It produces small, white flowers but does not possess a root.

Edibility: The nuts themselves are to be found beneath the water and are hard, greyish in colour and two-horned. These may be eaten raw, cooked with other vegetables, or roasted.

Bulrush (Typha spp.)
Distribution: Widespread.

Habitat: Shallow, fresh water and marshes. It can grow up to 4.5m (15ft) tall, and is distinguished by its large, long, dark brown flower head. It has long, narrow leaves which are grey.

Edibility: The edible parts are the rootstock, young shoots, leaves and pollen. The rootstock and young shoots can be eaten raw, but the leaves taste best when boiled. Pollen can be used to make damper bread. Bulrushes are also useful building materials for shelters, baskets, bedding, etc.

Flowering Rush (Butomus umbellatus)
Distribution: Common in Eurasia.

Habitat: This shallow-water plant grows up to 1.5m (5ft) tall and has long leaves rising from the base. It produces loosely clustered pink flowers with three petals.

Edibility: The edible part of the plant is the rootstock, found below ground. Should be peeled and boiled before being eaten.

Silverweed (Potentilla anserina)

Distribution: Wet ground in Temperate regions.

Habitat: A small creeping plant, it gets its name from the silvery-green colour of its soft, sharply serrated leaves, which are arranged alternately on a central leaf stalk. The flowers resemble those of the buttercup – yellow with five petals.

Edibility: The small creeping rootstock may be eaten, although many will need to be collected to make a meal. Luckily, silverweed usually appears in abundance. The roots can be eaten raw but are extremely astringent and taste better cooked.

Medicinal: An infusion of either the leaves or the plant will help in cases of diarrhoea, sore throat and stomach cramps. If applied externally it will soothe and heal wounds and haemorrhoids.

Silverweed

Arrowheads (Sagittaria spp.)

Distribution: Throughout many regions of the world.

Habitat: This aquatic plant can grow up to 0.9m (3ft) tall, and is distinguished by its large, glossy, arrow-shaped leaves which stand boldly above the water. Submerged leaves have a ribbon-like look to them. The flower stem rises from the root and carries small flowers composed of three white petals each.

Edibility: The edible part is the root tubers, which are the size of walnuts and grow just beneath the mud. They can be eaten raw but are much better when cooked. The roots are a source of vitamin C.

Reeds (Phragmites communis)

Distribution: Throughout many regions of the world.

Habitat: Freshwater aquatic plant, commonly found on river banks. A stout grass which can grow up to 3m (10ft) high, it has a creeping rootstock and grey-green leaves. The flowers, carried on the tall stems, are purple-brown in colour.

Edibility: The root, which is high in sugar content, can be cooked. The stem, if crushed, will yield a sugary gum which can be used for sweetening.

Seeds

All edible cereals are derived from wild grasses that produce heavy seed yields. A wide variety of grasses can be found in most regions, from the coldest tundra to all but the hottest desert. Although laborious to collect, the seeds will provide a basic food. They are best removed by simply gripping the seed head and pulling backwards so that the seeds fall into your hand. They can be collected in any improvised container, such as a hat or spare shirt. Once you have collected enough, rub the grain between your hands to loosen the chaff, and separate by throwing the whole lot into the wind, which will blow away the lighter chaff.

Wild grasses grow in many parts of the world, even as far north as the Arctic circle.

The seeds can then be ground into flour using a flat surface and round smooth stone. This flour can be mixed with either nuts or fruit, and baked into bread or biscuits.

Oil-Producing Plants

Sunflowers, poppies, olives and walnuts all produce oil which is both edible and can be used as fuel for lamps.

The poppy is one of the easiest flowers to recognized growing in the wild, and is almost always found in abundance. It favours recently broken ground. In moderation the seeds can be eaten raw with no ill effects, but they are best used to produce oil.

The seeds or fruit of any oil-producing plant need to beharvested and wrapped in cloth to make 'cheeses' (flat, round cakes); these are stacked on top of one another, and pressed. If using seeds, they are best cracked first on a smooth stone before being pressed. In a pure survival situation pressing presents a problem and some form of leverage needs to be

Preparation

Leaves, stems and buds are best boiled until they are tender. Keep replacing the water if your plant material has a bitter taste – this will reduce it.

Grains and seeds can usually be eaten raw, but most will taste better after being parched. Parching is usually done in a metal container, but can be done on a hot, flat stone on top of a Yukon Stove if no other container is available. Heat the grains or seeds slowly until they are well scorched.

Nuts are in most cases perfectly edible raw, but some, such as acorns, can be very bitter. These are best boiled for two hours and then soaked in fresh water for three or four days. All nuts can be ground up into a paste, which can either be added to soups or stews, made into a gruel, or dried into a 'flour' to make unleavened 'bread'. Sweet chestnuts (not to be confused with poisonous horse chestnuts or 'conkers') taste delicious whether roasted, baked, steamed or raw.

Fruit berries and soft fruits provide a welcome change to a survivor's diet. Both are best eaten raw as they contain many valuable vitamins which may be lost when cooked. Those fruits with thicker or tougher skins can be boiled, baked or roasted.

Sunflower seeds and poppy seeds can be eaten and also used to produce oil.

implemented. A press can be made if a vehicle jack is available.

The residual 'cake' is also edible, and is best rolled into biscuits and fried. Olives can be wrapped in a clean cloth and left out in the sun. The oil exudes into the cloth, which can then be wrung out. The cloth can then be used for lamp wicks.

Nuts

Nuts are an extremely valuable food source and can be found in most countries and climates except for the Polar regions. Nuts are extremely nutritious, providing high levels of protein, fats and vitamins. Tropical nuts include coconuts, brazil nuts and cashews, whereas trees in temperate areas produce hazelnuts, walnuts, beechnuts, acorns, almonds, sweet chestnuts and pine nuts.

If you have a plentiful source of nuts, gather as many as possible and store them in a cool, dry place. The nuts will remain edible for several months if left in the shell. Nuts are quite easily carried and make an excellent portable food store.

Fruits

Fruits, like nuts, are found in all climatic regions except for the most extreme. Fruits can be extremely high in vitamins and sugars, and often occur in plentiful amounts. Do not gorge yourself on wild fruits, however, as this

The brazil nut is contained within a large fibrous husk.

may well cause severe diarrhoea and sickness. What you can't eat at once, collect and dry. Make sure that you dry them thoroughly, however; otherwise they will become coated with harmful moulds and mildew. For the same reason, only pick and eat fruit that are healthy and not overly ripe.

Clamping Many root vegetables can be preserved through the winter by 'clamping'. A thick layer (20cm/8ins) of dry straw or bracken is used as a base onto which the tubers are placed in a pyramid. Cover the pile with more straw or bracken; and allow it to settle for two days before covering the whole pile with dry earth. It is a good idea to allow some strands of straw to protrude through the earth so that your 'clamp' may breathe.

Fungi

Fungi provide a nutritious and palatable wild food source, and they often occur in areas where other food resources are scarce. Only two to three per cent of fungi species are poisonous to human beings; and yet opinion is divided on advising their use as a source of survival food. The major problem arises from the fact that **THERE IS NO EDIBILITY TEST FOR FUNGI.**

This is due to the delay between poisoning and symptoms appearing, and also the exceptionally toxic properties of some species. Even species not considered poisonous can cause some extreme reactions in susceptible individuals who may have an allergy to them. Just because one person can eat a certain species quite safely does not mean that every member of a survival party can.

- Even though only a small percentage of fungi are poisonous to humans, some are extremely deadly – even if only a tiny portion is consumed.

- After eating a poisonous species of fungus the symptoms may not present themselves until ten to 40 hours later. By this time they will be serious enough to warrant hospitalization. In the worst cases, without hospitalization the casualty will die. Even with proper medical care irreversible damage may be caused to certain organs.

- Less poisonous species, although not fatal under normal circumstances, may cause poisoning serious enough to threaten the life of an already weakened person in a survival situation.

Identification of fungi

There is only one safe way to identify fungi, and that is by visual means. Make sure that you can positively identify certain species beyond doubt. Learn fungi identification by studying pictures from a good guidebook and comparing them to specimens found in the wild. Keep in mind that even reference books may disagree from time to time on whether a particular species is edible or poisonous. A decision to eat fungi must be based on sound knowledge and first-hand experience of identifying edible species, and where no alternative food source is available in the locality. If you are not able to do this, it is safer to leave fungi well alone.

Field Mushroom (Agaricus campestris) The Field Mushroom is similar in appearance to the Horse Mushroom except that it is not so large. It is found mainly in the summer on meadows and lawns, especially after rain.

The cap is white, convex, up to 12cm (4.75in) in diameter and sometimes covered in thin, smooth scales. The gills are free from the stem and densely packed together. The colour of the gills ranges from pinkish-red when young to black-brown later on. The stem grows to a height of 8cm (3ins) and is white and smooth. The flesh has a pleasant taste and smell. It can be fried or cooked in soups and stews.

Warning: The Field Mushroom looks extremely similar to the deadly Death Cap and Destroying Angel, especially when young, so be sure of your identification.

Bay-Capped Bolete (Boletus badius) The Bay-Capped Bolete has a convex cap, chestnut to dark red-brown in colour. The stem is a lighter colour, straight, thick and cylindrical, growing up to 8cm (3ins). It has olive-brown spores. It is found in deciduous and coniferous woods, and is extremely common. When cut or bruised the flesh turns blue. It can be fried, cooked on its own as a vegetable, or added to stews and soups. It can also be dried and stored for later use.

Cep or Penny Bun (Boletus edulis) The Cep is found in all types of woodland. It has a brown, convex cap 5-20cm (2-8ins) in diameter, which is thick and fleshy. It has a thick, cylindrical stem, which is usually white but can also be tinged with a pale brown and have a whitish network of veins. It has olive-brown spores. The cep is one of the few species that can be eaten raw; however, like the Bay-Capped Bolete, it can also be fried, added to soups and stews, or eaten on its own.

Warning: Do not eat any similar-looking mushroom with pink or red spores.

Sponge Cap (Boletus tes-taceao-scabrum) (Leccinum versipelle) Usually found growing with birch trees, this large mushroom often occurs in substantial numbers. It has a large convex cap, up to 15cm (6ins) in diameter and yellow-brown to orange-brown in colour. It has a

The Danger of Fungi

• Only a small percentage of fungi are poisonous to humans, but these are extremely deadly.

• Death can occur even if only a tiny portion is consumed.

• NEVER try testing fungi for edibility.

• Even less poisonous species, not usually fatal, may cause life-threatening sickness and weakness in a survival situation.

WARNING

**Full and confident recognition is the only safe way of
being sure whether a fungus is poisonous or not. There
are no other safe methods available. If you find yourself
forced to eat fungi, the following guidelines will give
some measure of safety:**

• **Avoid old specimens of fungi, or any that are diseased,
have insect infestations, or have been partly eaten by
insects or maggots.**

• **Avoid very young specimens, especially those that are
still in the 'button' stage. At this point many
fungi have not yet developed their identifying features –
these only appear as the fungus approaches maturity.**

• **Before picking any fungus, first examine it for any sign
of a volva or cup at its base. Picking a mushroom first
may destroy such evidence by damaging the volva or
leaving it in the ground. Any fungus possessing a cup or
volva at its base should not be picked or used in any
way.**

• **Similarly, avoid any fungus with a ring of scales on the
base of the stem, or if its cap is covered with small
white patches or fragments.**

• **Fungi with red on the underside of the cap, or which
produce red spores, should also be avoided.**

• **Leave any fungi that have white gills, or any gilled
mushrooms that have a milky-looking juice.**

• **Any fungus should be boiled before being eaten, and
the water should be discarded. This is because some
poisons are destroyed by cooking. However, there are
also other poisons, such as those found in the deadly
Amanitas, which are NOT neutralized by cooking.**

thick stem, growing from 7-15cm (2.75-6ins) tall. The stem is
white to grey and covered in dark woolly scales. The mushroom
has brown spores. The flesh is firm when young but softer later,
and can be coloured anything from white to pale pink to greenish-
blue depending on age. The Sponge Cap is not recommended for
soups, and is best fried or dried.

Buff Meadow Cup (Camarophyllus pratensis) This is to be
found in open aspects, such as woodland clearings or open
grasslands and meadows. It has a convex buff-coloured cap,
which later becomes more flattened in shape, often with a slight
dip or a centrally raised arch. The gills are the same colour as the
cap, thick and loosely arranged. The stem is slightly paler than the
cap, 3-8cm (1-3ins) tall, and widens at the top into the cap. It has

white spores. This mushroom can be either fried or stewed.

Horn of Plenty (Craterellus cornucopioides) This is easily recognized by its funnel-shaped fruit body, very dark brown in colour and rough and crinkled. It grows up to 10cm (4ins) in diameter and has a short, hollow stem. The Horn of Plenty is usually found in deciduous woodland amongst rotting leaves. The flesh is thin and spicy, and is best when mixed with others in soups and stews. It can also be fried.

Chanterelle (Cantharellus cibarius) Like the Horn of Plenty, this mushroom is also funnel-shaped, but is orange-yellow in colour and smells of apricots. In younger specimens, before the funnel forms, the cap is convex or flat. It has a short, pale stem and cream/pale red spores. It is to be found in woodland, especially under birches, although it also grows in coniferous woodland. The flesh is peppery to taste and is fairly indigestible unless it is chopped small and thoroughly cooked. This mushroom is not very good for drying.

Beef Steak Fungus (Fistulina hepatica) This leathery fungus grows on trees, usually oaks. It is rough in texture, and is red on the top with a paler pink underside. It has red flesh and a red juice. Older fungi tend to be bitter, so collect younger ones if available. Even then, the fungus will need to be soaked before being stewed.

Parasol Mushroom (Macro-lepiota procera) This mushroom occurs in deciduous woodlands and clearings. It has a large, brownish cap which is at first globular, but later becomes convex, and finally flat. Its diameter can be anything up to 25cm (10ins). The gills are white or cream, densely arranged and free from the stem. The stem grows from 15-30cm (6-12ins) high and is quite thin and pale brown in colour, with irregular dark brown bands around it. It has white spores. The flesh of the Parasol tastes nutty, like almonds or brazil nuts. The best method of cooking this mushroom is to discard the stem and fry the cap.

The closely related **Shaggy Parasol (Macro-lepiota rhacodes)** looks similar to the Parasol, but is smaller and has a shaggy-looking stem instead of the transverse brown markings. It is edible in the same way.

Common Puff Ball (Lycoperdon perlatum) The fruit body of the Common Puff Ball is very round to pear-shaped and is supported on a short, fat stem. The whole mushroom grows to about 5-8cm (2-3ins) in height and 4-7cm (1.5-2.75ins) in diameter. The fat cap is greyish white when young, later maturing to a yellow-brown colour, covered in small 'warts'. It has olive-brown spores. The flesh of this fungus should be eaten when it is still young and white, and is best fried.

Warning: Other related species may look similar but are inedible.

Giant Puff Ball (Calvatia gigantea) One of the largest fungi on earth, this mushroom looks like a giant football, up to 60cm (24ins) in diameter. It has smooth white skin and pure white flesh. It is found in woods and grassy places. It is delicious to eat and also has medicinal uses: the spores can stop bleeding from wounds and are also antiseptic.

Common Morel (Morchella esculenta) The Common Morel is often found where the soil has been disturbed, especially in grassy areas. The fruiting body is globular, yellow-brown and honeycombed in appearance. It can grow up to 20cm (9ins) tall. The stem is white or cream, cylindrical, and breaks easily. It has colourless to very pale yellow spores. The Common Morel has a white, waxy flesh which is very spicy-smelling. To cook, it is best to chop the flesh into small pieces first. It can also be dried.

Warning: The Common Morel must not be mistaken for the False Morel, which is poisonous.

Oyster Fungus (Pleurotus ostreatus) The Oyster fungus can be found growing on the bark of dead or living deciduous trees. It has a shell-shaped cap, flattish and usually brown in colour on the top. The gills are white but later turn more yellowish. The stem is very short, and hairy at the bottom. The Oyster produces large amounts of purplish spores. Collect only young fungi, as older ones tend to be tough. The flesh is soft and has a pleasant taste and smell. It can be fried or added to stews.

Common Blewit (Lepista personata) Found in open grassland, this variety usually grows in rings. It has a convex cap which later becomes flattened, buff in colour and about 6-12cm (2.5-4.75ins) in diameter. The gills are densely arranged and are white to pinkish-buff in colour. The stem is short, thick, and of a blue-lilac colour. This mushroom tends to appear in late autumn/early winter when most other varieties have disappeared.

It is best fried or stewed, but does not go well in soups.

Warning: Some individuals tend to have an allergy to the Common Blewit, so test with a small piece first.

Poisonous Fungi

Most poisoning by fungi is caused by species of one family – the amanitas, many of which are toxic to a fatal degree even in small quantities. The amanita family includes the Death Cap, the Destroying Angel, Fly Agaric and Panther Cap.

The amanitas share many common characteristics, such as possessing a cup or volva at the base of the stem; white gills; a smell of potato or radish; and fragments on the cap. Any mushroom possessing these characteristics should be avoided. Amanitas grow on their own and are only found in woodland – never in fields or open grassland. It is recommended that this family should be studied with the aid of a good guidebook for identification purposes.

Death Cap (Amanita phalloides) Young specimens are egg-shaped but later the cap develops convexity, and in maturity becomes flattened. The colour of the cap is pale yellow to olive-green with light lines leading from the centre to the edges. The stem is paler and possesses a volva at the base. The gills and flesh are white.

This fungus is found in woodland and is usually associated with oak trees. The flesh of young specimens possesses a sweet smell and a pleasant taste, but later the smell becomes less agreeable. This is one of the most poisonous of fungi and is fatal after consumption of even a small piece. The symptoms develop from one to three days after consumption; these include vomiting, sweating, excessive thirst, diarrhoea and convulsions.

Often the casualty will seem to make a brief recovery, but death soon follows, from acute liver failure. There is no known antidote for Death Cap poisoning.

Destroying Angel (Amanita virosa) This fungus shares a similar shape with the Death Cap, but its cap and stem tend to be pure white. The stem is more slender, shaggy, and tends to be slightly curved, but it still has the distinctive large volva at its base. The gills are white. The Destroying Angel is found in woodland, especially coniferous. It prefers mossy ground and will not be present in grassland. The flesh is white and soft and, like the Death Cap, has a sickly sweet smell when young. Older flesh has a less agreeable 'laboratory' type of odour. The symptoms and severity of poisoning are the same as for the Death Cap.

Panther Cap (Amanita pantherina) The Panther Cap is at first convex in shape but then flattens out and becomes cushion-like. The colour of the cap is a dull brown, and it is covered with white flecks. It has white gills and a white, smooth stem with a volva at the base which consists of two to three concentric rings. It is found in woodlands, particularly under beech. The white flesh often smells of raw potatoes.

Fly Agaric (Amanita muscaria) The Fly Agaric is easily recognized by its bright red cap covered with white spots – the original 'fairy mushroom'. This member of the amanita family tends to grow under pine or beech trees. Symptoms of Fly Agaric poisoning include vomiting and diarrhoea, dizziness, hallucinations and convulsions, followed by a coma-like sleep. Despite the seriousness of the symptoms, the victim usually recovers.

Devil's Boletus (Boletus satanas) This fungus is similar in appearance to the edible boletus edulis, but can be distinguished by certain differences. In younger specimens the cap is greyish-white and red at the edges, but more mature specimens have an ochre hue. The pores are blood red. The stem is coloured yellowish-orange above and purple below. Although poisonous, it is not usually fatal. Symptoms of poisoning include severe vomiting.

Inocybe patouillardii This fungus may be confused with an edible agaricus by a beginner. The cap is white in the younger specimen before it turns yellowish. The cap is often split at the edges. This mushroom stains red when bruised. Symptoms of poisoning include dizziness, sweating, blindness and a lowered temperature. In very severe cases the victim may become delirious and die.

Paxilus involutus This species is found in birch woodlands and is very common. It has a funnel-shaped, yellow-brown cap with a rolled rim, and yellow-brown gills. It may easily be confused with the Chanterelle, and is very toxic.

Animal Food

Mammals, birds, fish, reptiles, crustaceans and insects are all sources of animal food that can be found in the wild. Animal foods of any type will provide a higher food value than that obtained from plants; however, far more energy-sapping effort will be needed to catch an animal than to gather plants. Hunting and trapping all require time, skill, and good information. It is vital, therefore, that the result matches the cost of the methods employed. You must not expend more energy in catching the food than that derived from the food value caught.

Hunting Hints

The process of catching an animal is called hunting; this can be achieved by either trapping or pursuit. The first requires constructing some form of trap best suited to catch your animal; pursuit means to stalk or ambush an animal and kill it by direct means, i.e. stabbing, clubbing or shooting.

Traps can be constructed to catch just about any size of animal from a mouse to an elephant. If pursuing your prey or waiting in ambush you will need a weapon; this can range from a rock to a gun. A firearm will provide the best chance of successful hunting, with snares coming a close second. The construction and efficient use of primitive types of hunting weapon require a great deal of skill and practice.

Unless you are an expert, hunting with anything less precise than a rifle will probably produce little success; but lying in ambush will increase your chances.

- To be able to ambush your prey you will need to know where it lives and when it moves. Look for an animal trail, especially one that leads to water. Most animals will use these trails between their feeding and bedding grounds and their water source either in the early morning or in the late evening; so pick one as your time of ambush.

- Animals have more acute senses than humans, and are always on the alert for danger. Be patient; observe all potential prey; camouflage both your appearance and scent – daub mud over your face and hands. Keep a low, silent profile and use smooth, careful movement downwind while the animals are feeding. Find a good place to hide, and position yourself there well before any prospect of animal movement.

- Snares and nets work well when set around an area where an animal has been cleaned or butchered. The entrails will act as a very effective bait.

- Care must be taken when returning to a trap or a snare, as any wounded animal may be dangerous.

- A sharp whistle can stop rabbits and hares if startled into running. You may even be able to attract them to you by making a high-pitched kissing sound with your lips on the back of your hand to simulate a squeal.

- Birds should be watched to see if their movement will reveal a nest site containing nutritious eggs or young. These should never be overlooked as a food source.

- As a last resort, the survivor must consider eating anything that walks, flies, swims, crawls, creeps, jumps or wriggles.

- Where possible, try to use all of a carcass – do not discard anything without careful thought. Skins can be made into clothing; bones can be fashioned into arrowheads, fish hooks or needles; sinews and gut make good bow strings or sewing thongs.

Author's Note

It is my firm belief that there is no justification for hunting any animal for sport. Only within the context of this book do I advocate hunting, and then only as a matter of human survival under the laws governing nature – in as much that the strong and intelligent of any species will survive by preying on the less fit. Even in this situation the hunter must act responsibly, and not let any animal suffer unnecessarily. (All the dead animals pictured in this book were purchased dead from local country markets.)

Snares

Snares and traps are a far better alternative to hunting and ambushes, as they require less physical effort and time spent waiting. A well-made and correctly sited and set snare or trap will be effective 24 hours a day, without the need for constant vigilance. This method guarantees a 'cost-effective' meal in terms of the effort/benefit equation of survival. Start out by snaring small game; they are easier to trap, transport and prepare.

Always set several snares, but keep some distance between them; an animal caught in one snare will create enough noise to alert others to the possibility of danger. Make sure that all snares are checked on a daily basis – the caught animal may be your next meal, but there is no reason to let it suffer unnecessarily. If you are successful with any of your snares, collect the animal, kill it if necessary, and reset the snares for the next day.

Drag Snare If properly positioned the simple drag snare is a most effective way of catching a meal. Ideally the snare should be placed along a fresh run, in such a way that the animal's head will be caught. Tie the noose to a stake which has been driven firmly into the ground; or, if it is suspended above the run, secure it to a strong branch. To set the noose, position it so that its bottom edge is about 10cm (4ins – the width of the average hand) above the floor of the run; and adjust the noose until it is about the size of two clenched fists. If possible, encourage the rabbit or other animal into the trap by piling up dead twigs and branches on either side of the path leading up to the snare. However, do not make the mistake of using green twigs – the animal may consider these to be a distractingly tasty snack.

A properly used drag snare can be most effective.

Balanced Pole Snare The simple drag snare can be modified to make it even more efficient. A balanced pole snare will not only catch your prey, but will also lift it clear of the ground – out of reach of any other hungry predators or scavengers. This requires a suitable length of pole secured at its mid-point across the trunk of a nearby tree in such a way that the lighter end of the pole can be pivoted downwards directly above the animal run. Fix a snare firmly to that end of the pole. At the opposite end of the pole fasten a heavy rock to act as a counterweight. This counterweight should be heavy enough to lift your catch clear once the snare is activated.

Make a trigger by cutting interlocking notches in two pegs, which hold them together against straight line tension (i.e. when you try to pull them apart along the axis of the pegs) but which slip apart easily when disturbed sideways. Hammer one peg firmly into the ground at the side of the animal run. Attach your snare to the other, free peg; and also tie a line from this free peg to the light end of the pivot pole. Swing the light end of the pole down and hook the trigger halves together; check that they work smoothly. Check that you have set the noose at the correct height above the run and that the wire loop can move freely.

A simple trigger construction.

Spring Branch Snare A similar effect can be achieved by substituting a springy, bent-over branch from a nearby tree, or a bent-over sapling, for your pole and counterweight. Again, hold it bent down under tension by tying it to your notched trigger pegs and tying the

Figure Four Trap

1 Place your figure four trap where you see signs of animal activity.

2 Make sure that the bait is secured and that movement on it will trigger the trap.

snare to the free peg. If you intend using this method you are advised to check the spring strength of the branch beforehand, and adjust your trigger setting accordingly.

Hoop Spring Snare A hoop spring snare can be used where trees are scarce and you are forced to rely on small saplings. Using two saplings – either growing naturally close together, or cut down and firmly planted in the ground where you need them – bend them into an arch. The two tips are locked together by a notch which in turn is held in place by a vertical bait bar. (A rock can be attached to the bait bar if necessary, to supply the down-wards tension to lock the notch.) A number of snares are attached to the saplings and positioned in such a way that the animal must pass its head through a loop in order to get at the bait. Movement on the bait bar will trigger the trap and snatch tight the snares.

Whore Trap The whore trap relies on forcing the animal's head into a baited 'V'. A willow stick, sharpened at each end, is bent into a hoop and forced into the ground. The snare is fixed to the end of a bent-over sapling, or the end of a balanced pole snare. A bait stick is positioned so that the snare peg, which fits through the hoop, can rest on it. Two large logs or a series of stones form a barrier either side, forcing the animal to place its head through the snare before it can eat the bait. As the bait is taken the snare is activated. Of all the snare traps shown this is by far the most reliable.

Purse Net A simple purse net, if you have one, is another efficient way of catching small game. If you do not have one, make a gill net (see Fishing). The net can be used in several effective ways. First find a burrow showing signs of recent use, and stake the net over a fresh entrance. Block all of the other burrow holes except for one. In this hole either light a fire and blow smoke, or simply pour in water. Either method will make any occupants of the burrow panic, forcing them into the net.

Long Netting This is a simple and effective way of catching several rabbits at once. You will require a long net, which is placed between the burrows and the grazing ground. It is erected rolled up and balanced on several sticks; a cord is attached which allows the net to be drawn out. It is best used after dark when the rabbits are feeding. Stretch out your net, and then get behind the rabbits and make a lot of noise. The rabbits' first reaction is to bolt for their burrow.

Figure Four Trigger This type of trigger has the advantage of being easy to make, light to carry around with you, and capable of supporting any combination of useful traps. It is constructed from three lengths of thick branch, notched in such a way that they form a figure four. This trigger is firmly fixed in the ground where it will support a deadfall log or flat rock, or alternatively a drop net. Whichever method you choose, once the trigger is disturbed the trap will activate. The Figure Four Trigger is the ideal trap to use while travelling.

Squirrel Snares Once you have identified the presence of squirrels in an area it is fairly simple to catch one. The most effective way is to induce the squirrel to climb down a pole which is purposely positioned. Look for signs at the base of a tree to make sure squirrels are resident – pine cones husks, nut shells and bits of old mushroom are a good indicator. Fit three or four snares evenly spaced to a suitable pole about 4-5m (13-16ft) long. Place this against the tree, wedging it into a fork just below the foliage line. Any squirrels climbing the pole to their tree will run into the snares and be caught. A struggling squirrel will often attract others, who will come to investigate and then ensnare themselves.

Tin Can Trap One way to catch small animals is to dig a hole large enough to sink your billycan and

Snaring

The use of snares is discussed here purely in the context of survival; snaring animals is against the law in some countries, and is disapproved of in many others.

Making a Snare

The easiest type of snare, both to make and to use, is the drag snare, which kills by strangulation. A noose can be fashioned of any strong wire, nylon cord, hide strips, or even a wire saw (see Survival Kit). The best material to use is brass snare wire. You will need about 80cm (30ins) of wire for each snare. Make a 1cm (1/2in) loop in one end, passing the other end through the loop to make your noose. The pliability of the brass wire makes for a quick, smooth strangulation, which will lock in place as the animal struggles. Before setting it make sure that the wire is free of kinks and that the noose runs freely. Snares are best rubbed with animal excreta to remove the brightness of the metal and the human scent which your hands will leave on the wire.

The Simplest Rodent Trap

1 Find an established run used by small animals.

2 Dig a hole and sink a tin can below ground level.

3 Half fill the can with water.

4 Conceal the hole with grass.

half fill it with water. This is best done along the animal run, concealing the open top with grass. Most Arctic rodents feed on grass seed or moss, making them an attractive source of clean food.

Birds

All birds and birds' eggs are edible. Their taste depends on their habitat: those which live or feed at sea will be less palatable than those that feed on the land. The flesh from sea birds is nutritious but barely digestible, though this can be improved by thoroughly cooking it.

The normal indication of bird presence is simply to see them flying overhead, but many also leave signs near their nesting or feeding areas. Although it is difficult to identify a particular bird species by its track, you can still get a rough idea of the type of bird. By using the following simple guide lines you should be able to tell the difference between perching birds, swimming birds and wading birds:

- Perching birds (e.g. sparrows & crows) leave tracks with a long first toe (the gripping toe) behind three front toes.

- Swimming birds (e.g. ducks) leave webbed footprints.

- Wading birds have long slender toes spread wide apart. You will find their tracks in mud.

Bird Snares Birds can be caught in any number of ways, from throwing a stone to hitting them with a long stick. One of the simplest ways is to snare them. First find a perch that is well used by birds – this can easily be identified by the large amount of droppings either on the branch or on the ground below. The snares can then be hung above this branch. Once a bird has put its head through a loop it will not withdraw but will try to escape by flying forward, and thus become trapped.

Another method is by using the baited perch. If you have sufficient wire – at least 2m (6.5ft), make a snare loop at either end and fold them over a branch. Next form a square-ended perch with the trailing end onto which the birds are enticed to land. When a bird rests on the perch it will dislodge the whole snare, trapping the bird's neck at the same time. In most cases both

Bird and Fish Catcher

In isolated regions where man is rarely seen, most birds will remain perched and unafraid. Use a long gaff with a snare attached to hook your dinner.

bird and trap will fall to the ground.

Baited Bird Hook A simple baited hook (an open safety pin is ideal) can be used to catch larger birds such as seagulls, wild ducks and geese. These birds are greedy and swallow their food quickly. Make sure the line is well secured, and that you check all of your snares each day.

Bottle Trap Floating traps can be used to capture waterfowl while on the water. If you do not have a bottle use a small log instead. Half fill the bottle with water, and tie two or three snares to the neck so that they sit about 5cm (2ins) above the water. A little foliage will make the trap more attractive to any curious bird.

Unless the water is shallow and safe enough for you to wade in and retrieve the trap, secure it to the bank with a line so that you can pull in any catch.

Eggs Any survivor should keep an eye out for birds' nests; eggs offer high nutritional value, are convenient and safe, even if the embryo has developed inside. They can be boiled, baked or fried. Hard-boiled eggs can be carried as a food reserve, and if submerged in clean water will keep for several weeks. A thin coat of fat or grease around a fresh egg will keep it edible for a month or more. A survival diet of bird's eggs and boiled nettles will sustain life for a long time.

Never remove all the eggs from a nest; by leaving one or two you will encourage the bird to lay more. Mark those you leave, to ensure that you are removing only the fresh eggs.

Birds are easily trapped by rigging collapsible perches.

Preparation of Birds

Before cooking, birds need to be prepared by plucking and cleaning. Most birds can be plucked more easily either immediately after death, or after being plunged into boiling water. The exceptions to the latter are waterfowl, which are easier to pluck dry. Do not throw away clean feathers as these can serve many purposes, from insulation in bedding or clothing to making flights for arrows. Although it is possible to skin a bird, removing its feathers at the same time, remember that the skin will provide extra food value.

Once the bird has been plucked, cut off the head and feet and make an incision into the lower stomach below the breastbone. Use this hole to draw out the bird's innards and neck bone. (The heart, kidneys, liver and neck bone will form the basis of a good stew.) Wash the bird thoroughly, both inside and out, with fresh water. Small birds, once gutted and cleaned, can be enclosed in clay and baked on an open fire; the feathers and skin will pull away with the clay.

Carrion eaters – e.g. vultures, buzzards and carrion crows – are likely to be carriers of disease and parasites. They are still edible, but need to be boiled first for at least 20 minutes before you continue with any other form of cooking. Boiling will not only kill any parasites and bacteria present, but will also serve to make stringy meat more tender.

Traps for Larger Game

Scissors Trap A simple scissors trap features one log raised above another in a V-shape. The falling log is held in position by a trigger, and the direction of its fall is guided by stakes. It is essential that both trigger and retaining cord are strong enough to support the deadfall, yet upon activation will release quickly and smoothly. The falling log can be weighted to improve kill efficiency. One of the best trigger release systems is where two pegs or modified branches support a toggle attached to the release line.

The toggle itself should be baited to avoid the risk of the cord being chewed by the animal, and placed in a position where the animal must expose its neck in order to get at the bait.

Deadfall and Spears

A variation on the scissors trap is to cross the animal trail with a trip line, which when activated will drop either a log or weighted spears. *Note:* Many survival books illustrate this trap with the deadfall or weighted spears falling or swinging across the line of the path. Situating the fall to activate along the line of the animal trail will produce much better results.

Deadfall and spears.

Scissors Trap

1. Use guides to ensure your scissor trap closes correctly.

2. Weight the trap to ensure a clean kill.

3. Position the trigger and bait so that the animal is forced to commit itself correctly into the desired spot.

Baited Pit Constructing a trap by digging a hole takes a lot of energy, although there are times when the ground is soft and the surrounding area is habitat to the ideal catch. The jungle is just such an environment, and wild boar and pig the game.

Providing you have the means, you need to dig the pit at least 1m square by 1.5m deep (3.25ft square and 5ft deep). Placing sharpened bamboo stakes in the bottom may help disable the animal, but they are unlikely to kill it. Covering the pit so that it matches in with the natural surroundings is vital. Likewise, the support for the concealing cover needs to be firm enough so that it gives way only when the animal is 'centre stage' – this can be achieved by cutting part way through the supporting branches. Always approach an activated pit with care: injured animals can leave a nasty infected bite. Make sure your prey is dead by stabbing it with a spear before attempting to remove it from the pit.

Bait The use of bait will increase your chances of catching a meal, be it an animal or fish, but what you use as bait is important. The idea of baiting is to attract the animal by offering an easy meal, and to optimize the efficiency of the trap or snare. In the first instance the bait must be acceptable to the animal; there is little point in using a worm if the wet ground is covered with them. Conversely, strange-looking bait may make the animal wary. Almost all animals and birds are attracted to blood, brightly coloured berries, and salt.

Hunting with a Weapon

Most improvised weapons, whether hand-held or projectile, require the addition of a cutting or piercing blade or edge. These can be fashioned from a wide variety of materials. Stone can be chipped to form an edge, and flint is particularly good for making weapons. Shave wood with a knife into a point and harden by charring slightly over a fire. Some woods, like bamboo, are naturally hard and only need trimming to a point. You can use man-made materials such as metal and glass to produce a good cutting edge.

AR-7 Survival Rifle Though it is rare nowadays to find a rifle packed in a survival kit, they do exist, and in certain environments prove most useful for hunting. Most survival weapons are of small calibre, since the relatively devastating ammunition used on the battlefield is unnecessary for hunting. The popular AR-7 survival rifle fires a .22 Long bullet. The AR-7 conforms to the needs of a survival situation, since it packs down for carriage into its own hollow stock, is lightweight, and will even float in water. Its 20-round magazine should, if used with sensible economy, supply sufficient meat to last several months.

The weapon is semi-automatic, which means it will fire a round each time you pull the trigger, i.e. you are not required to cock the weapon each time. For this reason, be careful not to let your trigger finger 'run' – aim for one round, one kill. Try to shoot an animal that will provide a good amount of meat, such as a fox, wild pig or capybara. Rabbits and birds can be caught by snare and are a waste of ammunition. Conversely, if you hunt game that is too large, such as a moose or bear, you will only wound it – which is wasteful of ammunition, cruel, and often extremely dangerous.

Assembling the AR-7 is simple:
- Open the rear of the stock, and empty out the parts.
- Slot in the trigger housing and bolt action assembly.
- Match up the barrel and body notches and secure with the screw collar.
- Check all parts are hand-tight; then fit the magazine.

Balala Light

'Balala light' is an African term for hunting with a light. A powerful torch is attached to a helmet or hat and aligned with the eyesight. When game are near the light is switched on, illuminating both the animal and the gun sights. The animal is temporarily frozen by the bright light, and is easily killed.

Zeroing Under survival conditions ammunition may be limited to one full magazine (20 rounds). If the rifle is inaccurate, you could miss with every shot. You are advised to test the rifle by firing three rounds at a large target.

From a distance of 50m (55 yards), fire at the same fixed point each time. Estimate an imaginary point at the centre of your three bullet holes, and measure the distance and angle from your fixed point. If the centre of your group is left 5cm (2ins) and slightly high, you need to aim off to the right by the same distance and slightly low. Aiming off is better than adjusting your sights, as you will need to confirm any adjustment by firing more ammunition. Always aim at the centre shoulder area of the animal.

Bow and Arrow Providing you can locate the correct materials it is possible to make a good hunting bow in a fairly short time. The most important part of the process is to select your stave – the part that forms the arc of the bow. Select carefully, choosing a strong, healthy section of wood without side shoots. The most traditional wood to use is yew, but oak, birch and hickory are all suitable. The wood should be long enough to make a bow stave about 130cm (50ins) in length.

Flex your stave several times to find which side bends naturally. Mark this side, and taper off the last 50cm (18-20ins) at both ends. Traditional English bow makers always tapered their bows to a round section and made the ends as even as possible – this was to stop the bow twisting when it was drawn. The bow stave should be slowly dried over a fire for about two or three days. Notch the ends to receive the bowstring.

To string the bow use whatever strong cord you have to hand; parachute cord will do. One alternative is to use cleaned animal intestines dried and twisted together to form a string. Tie the string on to one end of the bow only. Make a loop in the other end so that it can be slipped over the other end when the bow is flexed. The bow should only be strung like this when you intend to use it; at all other times it should be left untensioned.

Stringing a bow

Making a Bow

❶ Select a hardwood staff about 1.3m in length that is free of knots and limbs. Chamfer a third of the length at each end.

❷ Notch both ends to receive the bow string.

❸ String the bow by securing one end and forming a slip-over loop on the other.

Arrow shafts Arrows are made from straight, strong wood about 65cm (25ins) long and 1cm (0.4in) in diameter.

Most types of wood will do, but choose birch saplings if you can find them. Clean any bark off the arrow and straighten it as much as you can – a good method is to gently chew the arrow between the teeth. Remember – a straighter arrow will fly further and hit with greater force. Balance the arrow on your finger at its halfway point. Insert your flight in the lighter end and the arrowhead at the heavier. At the flight end cut a notch about 6mm (0.25in) deep to take the bowstring – check the width against your string material.

Arrow flights.

Arrow flights Arrows need flights – 'feathers' – in order to keep them on course when shot. They can be fitted with double or treble flights, and these can in practice be made from actual feathers or plastic, polythene or cardboard. The flights should be 10cm long and 5cm wide (4ins by 2ins). In a survival situation a one-piece double flight is best used.

Using a knife or other thin blade, carefully make a split about 15cm (6ins) long into the flight end of the arrow shaft. Insert a double flight into this – i.e. a single piece which protrudes equally on either side of the shaft. If the arrow splits completely, bind the split ends together tightly with light cotton, fish line or very fine snare wire.

Arrowheads A variety of arrowheads can be made using different materials, but all are attached in a similar manner to the flights: carefully split the shaft, insert the head, and bind the split shaft tightly. If you can find nothing to act as an arrowhead, harden the tip of the shaft by turning it slowly in a fire. Once hardened, any charred material should be removed and the tip sharpened to a point.

Blow Pipe Although most people think of the blowpipe as a weapon used by jungle tribes, it is possible to construct a very effective modern-day variation which can be used for hunting small game such as birds and rabbits. Most of the materials required can be found in any modern vehicle or aircraft. For example, the body of the blowpipe can be constructed by simply cutting out a length of fuel pipe. Choose a section that is straight and at least 1.5m (5ft) in length; if this is not

Improvised arrow heads.

A blowpipe in use.

possible, try joining two or three shorter sections together. More air will be forced down the pipe if a mouthpiece is fitted at one end; this can be cut from card or plastic and held in place with ducting tape.

Metal darts between 10 and 15cm (4-6ins) long are constructed from stiff wire. Heat one end in a fire until it is glowing red, then flatten it to form a point by beating. Allow it to cool or dip it in water. The flight can be made from any soft, pliable material, e.g. seat foam or polystyrene. Use a short section of pipe which has the same diameter as your blowpipe to stamp out your flights; this will ensure an airtight fit, while allowing the dart to be blown easily through the blowpipe. Shooting with your blowpipe needs no explanation, other than to say that your accuracy will become second nature after a little practice. The example illustrated here has a range of 25m (80ft), and is capable of killing a rabbit.

Slingshot The slingshot is a very simple weapon, easy both to make and, with practice, to use. Take two equal lengths of cord or leather about 35cm (14ins) long, and attach one end of each to a small, shallow pouch of fabric or leather which will hold a walnut-sized pebble. Tie a loop in the opposite end of one cord, and a knot at the end of the other.

Place the loop over the index finger of your dominant hand, and trap the knot between index finger and thumb. Place your ammunition securely in the centre of your pouch - ideally this could be a small, smooth pebble. Bring the sling above your head in one quick swinging motion to gain momentum. Let go of the knot to release the stone. You do not need to swing the sling more than a couple of times. Try using a flicking action to improve accuracy.

Throwing Stick Used properly a throwing stick is a most effective

LIFESAVER

AVOID using your knife as a spearhead unless there is a very good reason to do so. You are liable to damage your blade – or, worse still, lose it altogether. Its value to you in any survival situation is far greater than that of a spearhead, which can be made quite easily from chance-found or naturally occurring materials.

The Bolas

1 Attach evenly sized rocks to three bits of strong cord.

2 Wind up above your head.

3 The stones will separate as you throw them at your prey.

means of knocking down and stunning a running animal. It is best to cut several 50cm (20in) lengths of heavy fist-sized sticks for throwing. Hurl them overhand or by side-throw, using a flicking motion on release to make the stick spin through the air. Advance on the animal the moment it is down, and club it to prevent undue suffering.

Club The club is probably rivalled only by the picked-up stone as the oldest known weapon. In its basic form it will extend the range of your arms and deliver a more powerful hit than your fist. Clubs can be made from either wood, stone or metal, and can be weighted or formed into a 'mace'. Construction of any club should be designed around its planned use and the ability of the user. Making a club will protect the survivor against some larger animals, such as wild dogs; and will also serve to ensure a clean kill of any animal caught but struggling in a trap.

Bolas The bolas is a very effective weapon for bringing down large, long-legged animals such as deer, wild sheep or ostrich. It is simply made, comprising three lengths of strong cord knotted together at one end and weighted with stones at the other ends. The stones should be of even weight and no larger than a duck egg.

Practise on a nearby tree by swinging all three lines above your head. When you let go of the knotted end the lines will separate and wrap around your target. Be ready to spear your game the moment it is down, as the bolas will not immobilize it for long.

A catapult can be used effectively with arrows as ammunition.

Catapult If you have the means to make a catapult under survival conditions it will prove to be a highly effective hunting weapon. All you need is a strong, forked twig and a length of elastic (you might even consider putting some into your survival kit). A good source is the rubber taken from a vehicle's inner tube. Avoid clothing elastic, as this is generally too weak for the purpose. Construction is simply a matter of tying the ends of the elastic to the forks of your Y-shaped twig and the other ends to a good-sized projectile pouch – tie them tightly, and make sure the pouch is centred.

If you have a good length of elastic available, try using an arrow instead of a stone. Once this method has been perfected you will find it both more accurate and more deadly.

Spears Spears are useful for protecting yourself against an attack by a wild animal, but they are of less use for hunting. To make an efficient throwing spear and achieve consistent accuracy demands skills of a high order. A thrown spear is less accurate and projects less killing power than an arrow. For hunting a spear can really only be used against cornered prey, although fishing spears are of more value.

To make a spear, choose a strong staff about 180cm (70ins) long and sharpen the end. If you have the materials and the time, experiment by making spearheads from other materials, such as flint, or metal or glass from a vehicle or aircraft.

Spears

1 Spears with multiple barbed heads are best for fishing.

2 Split the shaft to attach a metal or stone head.

Animals to Hunt: Tracks

Whether or not you actually see a prey animal, you can try to identify and locate it by studying and following its tracks. Efficient tracking is a highly sophisticated skill, and acquiring it in a survival situation will present a considerable challenge to most people.

One animal's track can look like that of a completely different animal depending on the surface on which it is imprinted. Sand, mud and snow will alter the image of an animal's footprint. You will rarely find a perfect print with the elements against you. Snow thaws and rain will wash away mud, resulting in a distorted shape. Even if you are convinced that you are trailing one type of animal, it could still turn out to be another. There is always a chance that a young animal could leave a print like a smaller creature. The different tracks made by fore feet and hind feet can trick you into thinking you are following the tracks of a different animal.

With all this against you, you need to have a clear idea of what to look for in the first place. Your conclusion should not be based purely on the print, but also on your surroundings. You should be considering what type of surface the track has been made in; the time of day or night; the weather conditions which may have affected the print; and, most important of all, the probable game in your particular surroundings. There are generally other clues, too.

As an example of similar tracks, consider a rabbit and a squirrel.

Tracks

• Study your environment at length, and use your common sense. What animals are likely to leave tracks here? Where are they going, and why?

• How is the surface – sand, mud, etc. – affecting the tracks?

• Is the weather affecting the tracks?

• Is this a full-grown small animal, or a young larger animal?

• Can you tell the front from the rear prints?

• If so, do the tracks tell you anything about the speed of movement?

• Are there any other tell-tale signs – droppings, or chewed vegetation?

The rabbit will push off with its hind feet and land on its fore feet, which touch the ground one after the other. The hind feet then touch the ground landing in front of the fore feet. This leaves a print of the larger hind feet, followed by the print of the smaller front feet. The squirrel has a similar type of movement, with the hind feet landing in front of the fore feet, leaving the same type of print. It would be very difficult to decipher which footprints had been left by which animal – if it were not for one simple clue. A squirrel's trail starts and ends at a tree.

A series of tracks will give you a trail which gives you an idea of the speed at which an animal was moving. The greater the gap between the groups of tracks the faster the movement. A walking animal moves its right fore foot first, followed by the left hind foot. Then the left fore foot is moved, followed by the right hind foot, and so on. A trail made by a walking badger will show that the hind foot has landed on the track of the fore foot. This is called 'being in register', and is what happens when an animal has been walking or trotting – it moves its legs in a definite order. If an animal has been galloping, the tracks will not be in register.

Rabbit Rabbits deserve a special mention; they are a great source of wild food, and are found on every continent living in all conditions, from Arctic to desert. They are easily recognizable, and being a social animal are always found in large numbers. They usually stay in one territory all their lives, where they live in burrows, often with more than one entrance. They are most prevalent in open grassy areas and open woodlands, especially where the soil is dry and sandy. Burrow sites are made in banks and slopes with light tree or shrub cover.

The tracks that rabbits regularly use are called runs. These are easily seen between the burrow entrances and, if in present use, will have rabbit droppings on them – small, dark, round 'currants'. When you set a snare make sure that it is a little distance from the burrow entrance itself – animals are far more wary when emerging from underground than at most other times, and a snare set too close to the entrance may well be seen by the rabbit and avoided. Take care not to disturb the ground or foliage around the run when setting the snare, and conceal your scent by rubbing the snare and your hands with animal droppings.

A live rabbit is best killed by holding its hind legs in your left hand and its neck in your right. Stretch and twist the neck sharply until the neckbone breaks; death will be instantaneous.

Deer Deer can be found from the lower Arctic to the lower reaches of the jungle. They walk on two toes, leaving a definitive track. They live in open country and woods. Many have branched antlers, which they drop after the October rut – the mating time for deer and other hoofed animals. Red deer start off as spotted calves; during the summer their coats change to a red/brown colour. Their diet consists of grass, fruit, heather and tree bark; it is also not unknown for them to raid crops.

Elk and Moose These are large deer, their coats ranging from grey/brown to black in colour. They live mainly solitary lives, but can live in small groups. Their habitat is open forest, especially close to water (they are very good swimmers). Marshlands make an ideal setting for them in the summer, although they often move to drier ground in the winter months. Their diet includes leaves, young shoots, water plants, grass and moss.

Wild Goat These have horns with a simple, gentle curve which can grow up to 1m (3.25ft) long. They tend to have a shaggy coat in the winter months, and live in small herds on open hillsides. They are found in the uplands of North and South America, Europe and Asia. Their diet includes grass, leaves, lichen and moss.

Wild Boar The adult wild boar has a dense, dark-coloured coat, although youngsters are striped. They have a long snout and the male has large tusks, which can grow up to around 30cm (12ins) long. The male lives a solitary life except in the rut. They live in deciduous woodlands and marshes of North America and Europe, and in the tropical forests of South America and Asia. Their diet includes roots, bulbs and fallen fruit. Boar can be very dangerous; despite their size they are able to attack humans, being fast, heavy and aggressive. Wild boar are heavily infested with worm.

Fox The fox's coat varies from sandy to a dark chestnut colour. The red fox has a bushy tail, usually with a distinctive white tip. Their preferred habitat is woodland, although they are very

Trapping vs. Hunting

• Hunting demands practised skills – silent movement, concealment, reading the natural environment, predicting animal behaviour. Survivors from urban backgrounds rarely have them. All potential prey animals do.

• Trapping demands the ability to visualize basic mechanical principles, to fashion simple materials, and to study the surroundings. These are skills which even urban adults can master well enough to deceive most animals

• Hunting means movement, sometimes over long distances. This expends the survivor's energy. If he is unsuccessful, it is not replaced.

• Making and setting traps and snares demands little strength, and less movement across country – therefore less energy loss.

• The hunter normally has to focus on a single prey. If that prey escapes him, his time and energy have been wasted.

• The trapper can set many snares, all of which are potentially working for him simultaneously and for 24 hours every day. They are dramatically more productive by the equation of cost against possible rewards.

adaptable and will live in built-up areas. They are usually nocturnal, and are active all year round. Their natural diet includes young deer, small mammals, birds, poultry, grass and fruit. They normally live in a single-entrance burrow, making them easy to catch if you dig them out. **Warning: Many foxes carry rabies.**

Rodents Rodents belonging to the subspecies known as myomorpha make up about a quarter of all mammals. The best known of these animals are the various types of rats and mice. They have adapted themselves to surviving in almost any location except for Antarctica and colder regions of the Arctic. Their diet consists of seeds and other vegetation; but certain species have become omnivorous, and will eat any food left out by humans.

The problem for the survivor is that rodents are the carriers of many diseases – leptospirosis, rabies, ratbite fever, murine typhus, bubonic plague, hantavirus and spirochetal jaundice, etc. Through their urine, droppings and hair food can easily become contaminated, and at the very least will pose a threat of bacterial food poisoning. Despite this, the animals are edible. This makes them a ready source of food, and one which mankind has often turned to, especially in times of famine.

Hamster In the West these have become popular pets, known for their docile nature. However, in their native environment in the Middle East, Russia, China and some areas of Europe they are often considered a pest, as they can cause serious damage to crops. They live in chambered burrows which can be found 20-30cm (8-12ins) below the surface of the ground. Being a naturally solitary animal, the hamster will defend its territory aggressively against any other hamster, and will even fight during mating. The normal diet mainly consists of seeds, leaves, roots and fruit.

Norway Rat The Norway or Common Rat actually originated in eastern Asia, making its way into Europe at some time during the Middle Ages. This rat can be distinguished from others of its species by its blunter nose, smaller ears and shorter tail. It is a very adaptable animal, capable of living either in the wild or urban habitats, but its preferred environment is a wet or damp one. In its natural state it will live along river banks or beaches. The Norway rat is a burrowing animal; its burrows will often be up to half a metre (18ins) deep and will have several entrances and chambers. Small family groups inhabit these chambers. These rats tend to have small territories and, as long as there is enough food, will stay within their boundaries. They are creatures of habit and will follow the same foraging trail each time they go to seek out food.

Jerboas Jerboas are desert-living rodents, able to cope with the high temperatures and aridity of their native regions of North Africa and Asia. Their bodies are small, with disproportionately large hind legs and feet enabling them to jump great heights and long distances. Their fore feet are smaller, with strong claws so that they can dig out their burrows at the edges of sand dunes. They have long, tufted tails which act as a balancing aid when they jump and also as a support when they stand upright. Jerboas have very broad heads and large eyes, which help them to see in the dark; during the day they remain in their burrows with the entrances blocked to prevent any unnecessary evaporation of water. Like most desert animals, jerboas receive all their water requirements from the food they eat.

The Preparation of Animals

Skinning and dressing an animal carcass will be much easier if it is done as soon after death as possible. First the carcass should be bled. Smaller and medium-sized animals can be hung upside down from a frame, with the ropes attached around the hocks. The throat should be cut and the blood collected in a container below. Do not throw away this blood; it contains many valuable vitamins, minerals and salt, and once it has been boiled thoroughly it can be used as a food source. It is ideal for thickening and adding flavour to soup.

Note: If you catch an extremely large animal such as a moose or bear, which is impossible to haul up for butchering, you should consider moving your camp to the beast rather than trying to carry it back piecemeal.

Preparing Rabbits   Rabbits and small members of the cat family can provide a survivor with a relatively easy-to-catch source of meat. However, rabbits lack the fats and vitamins needed to sustain a survivor's health. Be aware that although a rabbit-rich diet may be easy and tasty, it can also lead to severe malnutrition over a period of time.

When skinning a rabbit, first make a cut behind the head and make sure that it is large enough to insert two fingers. Peel the skin back and cut off the head and lower limbs. To gut the carcass, cut a line down the belly and open out the body. Most of the innards should fall out when you give the carcass a sharp shake, but make sure that any remaining pieces are scraped out with a knife and washed away with fresh water.

Preparing Rodents   Rats and mice are not only edible; they are delicious when stewed with dandelion leaves or other kinds of vegetable. Skin, gut and wash them in the usual way; but boil them for about ten minutes before any other form of cooking, to destroy any parasites or bacteria they may be harbouring.

Preparing Hedgehog, Porcupines etc   Animals that have a protective coat of spines or a thick shell are best rolled in a thick layer of clay and cooked in the embers of an open fire. Make sure that these animals, especially large ones, are cooked all the way through; any sign of blood when you open it means it is not

Preparing a Rabbit

❶ As with most animals, cut around the leg joints below the thigh.

❷ Make a centre cut from the neck down to the stomach.

❸ Cut down both legs to allow you to remove the fur in one piece.

❹ Remove gut and press down on the bladder before removing fur.

cooked properly. Crack and remove the clay; the spiny skin will pull off with it to reveal the flesh. Eat only those parts you are familiar with, keeping the rest for bait.

Preparing Insects   To humans, insects are not the most appetizing food source; yet any survivor would be foolish to overlook their potential. They are the most plentiful life form on earth, and pound for pound, provide twice the amount of protein as steak.

Insects live both above and below ground; in either case their nests are easily found. Rotting logs provide homes for grubs, termites and beetles. Large flat stones make good nesting sites for a whole host of different species. Remember that insect larvae are also edible and highly nutritious.

Warning: A few insects are best left alone. These include any which are brightly-coloured or hairy, and those that carry disease such as ticks, flies, and mosquitoes. Some adult insects will bite, and those with hard-shell bodies can harbour parasites.

Almost all insects are found in abundance, so their small individual size is of little consequence – the mass will provide enough protein. The appearance of insects is also of little importance other than providing the means to recognize its suitability for eating. The secret of dealing with insects lies in how they are prepared.

This is best done by collecting as many as possible – a minimum of several cupped handfuls. These should be placed in a metal container which has been preheated over a hot fire (a lid of some sort will stop the more active species from crawling out).

It will take several minutes for them to cook, and it is best to turn and shake the container in order to toss the insects and prevent them from burning. Once all the insects are inert, leave them to dry further beside the fire. A good test is to pick an insect from the container and crush it between your fingers; the whole body should disintegrate to a dark brown dust. Next, grind the cooked insects using a stick as a pestle. When this is done pour the powder into a container of warm water; this will separate any unpulverised wings and legs, which will float on the surface where they can be removed. The remaining liquid is little more than a tasteless protein soup, to which edible plant parts can be added to make a nourishing meal.

Butchering Larger Animals

Once your deer, pig, wolf, etc. has 'bled out', the carcass can be skinned:

❶ Make the first cut around the knee and elbow joints. Carefully make a full circular cut around the genital organs. Then, starting at each knee, cut the skin down to the abdomen, forming a V-shaped cut.

❷ Continue cutting down the front of the animal, stopping at its neck. Be careful not to pierce the abdominal wall beneath, as this will spoil the skin. To protect the abdominal wall from the knife, place your hand behind the cut, inside the carcass.

❸ Make two more cuts from the front elbow joints in towards the belly.

❹ Return to the hind legs and peel back the skin; a cutting and pulling action is best. Continue until the skin has been completely removed.

❺ Cut open the abdominal membrane – without piercing the stomach or other organs – down to the chest bone. Use wooden skewers to pin back the flaps. Much of the gut will fall from the stomach and drop onto the ground.

❻ Check that you have removed all internal organs, starting with the windpipe and moving upwards. To clear the entire mass, use a knife to make a deep circular sweep around the genital organs; avoid cutting the bladder.

❼ After inspection for any signs of disease, keep back the parts of the offal which will be useful (e.g. the kidneys, liver, heart, and the fat surrounding the intestines). Use the rest of the innards for bait, or to make sewing gut. Also keep back the meaty parts of the skull; the brain, eyes and tongue are all edible.

❽ Once you have cleaned and prepared the meat the skin can be cleaned and dried in order to preserve it.

FISHING

Of all the aquatic foods, fish are the easiest to catch and offer the most obvious form of nourishment. Even with the crudest of fishing equipment, as long as you have knowledge and patience you will be able to catch enough fish for your needs. As with most things, catching fish is a skill and requires practice, and it is unlikely that you will catch much on your first attempt. With growing experience, patience, and the ability to vary your methods according to the situation, you will find a fishing technique which will achieve the results you want.

There are not many general rules that apply to fishing, as they can be caught by a variety of methods – hooks, nets, traps, snares, spears, stunning, poison, and even by simply using bare hands to grab them. All species differ in their feeding habits; however, it is generally accepted that most fish will take bait at dawn and dusk – look for the signs of feeding at those hours. Big fish are hard to catch as they are heavy and full of fight; if you do not have the correct fishing kit in your survival pack, then improvise. If you see large fish close to the surface try using a spear or bow and arrow, stalking your fish with extreme care in order to get close enough.

When and Where to Fish

In hot weather fish will tend to seek cooler water, either in deeper river pools or under shade; these are the places in which to cast for fish. The outer bank of a river bend also holds deeper water and this may be a good place to fish, especially if water levels are running low. Deep lakes are also good bets in hot weather. Fish tend to shelter below underwater rocks and logs or undercut riverbanks.

In cooler weather, or at dawn and dusk, fish tend to prefer shallower water or can be found around the edges of a lake or pond. Fish need a certain amount of warmth and will seek out warmer water. They also tend to feed better in shallow water. Fish will always lie in the water facing the oncoming current. This enables them to spot any food coming towards them, and also ensures a better flow of water over their gills. Knowing this, you will have better success if you let your natural bait move downstream towards likely shelter spots at a natural pace, so that they can see it and hopefully accept it as a normal piece of food.

Fish also like to be where the water is well aerated, such as at the bottom of a small waterfall. When using natural bait, cast it into the cascading water and let it move naturally down and across the pool, or for a little distance downstream if in moving water. Then, very smoothly and quietly, bring the line in and cast again as

Look for Fish:

In warm weather:
• In deep pools and lakes.

• Under shade, and undercut banks.

• On the outside of bends In cool weather, and at dawn and dusk:

• In shallows.

• Round the edges of ponds and lakes.

In any weather:

• Under white water.

before. The best pole to use for this type of fishing is a slender, flexible one, as this enables the line to be pulled gently out of the water instead of being dragged back through it. This type of pole also makes casting and recovery a lot less effort for the angler. If you are fishing for carp, catfish or eels you need to be aware that they feed on the muddy beds of slow-moving rivers and ponds. With this in mind, bait will need to be cast on the bottom and then moved very slowly.

Bait Your first choice for bait should be food that is normal to the fish's diet. Before you start to fish on a stretch of water, study it and the surrounding shore for morsels normal to the fish. Look for insects, worms, shrimps, minnow or shellfish. If none of this natural bait is available you will have to substitute an alternative, such as small scraps of meat or artificial substitutes. Fish are often attracted by the struggles of live bait. Try using a grasshopper or a beetle and see if it is taken by a fish. If it is, take another insect and carefully impale it on the hook without killing it. This should attract another bite from the fish, which this time will end up being caught. Minnows can also be used as bait in this manner, but under the water. The hook should pass through the body under the backbone and to the rear of the minnow. A float will be needed to keep the bait off the bottom of the water.

Lures and Hooks A lure is some form of artificial bait. It is designed to look like an insect or a small fish in order to fool the fish

Fish Hooks

❶ A simple bait covered gore.

❷ Stiff wire or safety pin.

❸ Whittled hardwood.

❹ Strong dog rose or similar thorn.

Improvising a fish hook can be simpler than it seems.

into thinking that what it sees is its natural food. A convincing appearance alone is not enough; the angler must also be able to manipulate the lure in order to mimic the movements of live bait struggling in the water. Lures can be improvised from many sources of material. They can even be made from a tuft of hair (from your own head if necessary), feathers, a scrap of brightly coloured cloth, or a fish fin with a piece of flesh attached. In fact, anything will do as long as it looks like an insect of some description. The lure should be constructed around the hook so that this is hidden.

Your basic survival fishing kit should contain a good supply of variously sized hooks. Good fishing hooks can also be improvised from a wide variety of materials and items – thorns, safety pins, wire, etc. Always make sure that your hook is the correct size for the fish you are trying to catch; and that, once you get a bite, the hook will stay attached to the line.

Commercial and improvised lures.

Fishing Hints

Fish tend to be very wary, and will swim away and hide at the first sign of anything they perceive not to be in their normal pattern of events. They are able to detect even the slightest vibration in the water, and are even aware of heavy footfalls on the bank. Therefore it is vital that when you approach the edge of the water you do so slowly and gently to keep any ground vibration to a minimum. Keep as low as you can, as quiet as you can, and move as little as possible. Never let your shadow fall onto the water.

Put your bait into the water slightly upstream from the location of the fish, and allow it to drift downstream with the current until it has passed you. If by that time no fish has taken the bait, gently recover it and try again. If no fish take the bait after a few tries, change your fishing pitch – but remember to make your move slowly and quietly. If you still are having no luck, try again at the opposite end of the day, or even after dark if the water is clear and shallow.

Night Line

❶ A float will indicate when you have a bite.

❷ The addition of a weight will allow you to determine what depth your bait is.

Portable Fish trap

1 Portable fish traps should be woven according to the size of fish you are trying to catch.

2 Place in the water with the mouth facing upstream.

Attracting Fish Attracting fish to a feeding ground is a good way to ensure a bite. Many anglers throw ground bait into the water to lure fish into what they perceive to be a good feeding ground. If you have plenty of bait it is recommended that you do the same. An alternative method when fishing in a pond, pool or lake is to tie a piece of unwanted offal or carrion to a branch overhanging the water. This will attract blowflies to lay their eggs in the meat. After a few days maggots will appear, and will fall into the water at a steady rate, thus attracting the fish. If you then place one on your hook you should soon catch something; better still, use a large net.

Night Line Fishing A night line consists of a line with one or more hooks which is left in the water all night. The hooks (preferably gorge hooks) should be baited with something that cannot easily be lifted off by eels, such as a small fish or a small piece of meat. The line should then be fastened firmly to a rock or a stake on the bank or an overhanging branch. The line should be checked every morning for a catch; if there is one, remove it and replace the bait. The line can have a single hook, or several stretched on a line across the river. The depth of the hook can be adjusted with weights to catch a variety of fish under most conditions.

Fish Traps Fish traps can be used in both fresh and sea water. The type of trap required will be dependent on the water in which you are fishing and the size of the fish. Traps can be made to be portable or permanent. The most common form of fish trap is the portable basket type, built with a cone-shaped entrance. They can be constructed from hazel or willow sticks, reeds or bamboo, or improvised from man-made discarded containers such as a plastic bottle. This shape makes it easy for the fish to get in and almost impossible to escape. Once constructed, the pot should be baited and placed facing upstream in a river or a rock pool.

Permanent Traps An on-site trap can be made by piling stones or driving wooden stakes into the riverbed to form a pen. It may be necessary to form the trap in such a way that fish will be funnelled through the entrance into a secure compound. The siting of the trap is critical, but where possible full advantage should be taken of natural features which will enhance your catch and save time and energy. It may be possible to herd fish by wading into the water starting 100 metres upstream and walking towards the trap. Trapped fish can be speared with a sharp stick.

Fish Pen

1 Fish funnelled through entrance to pen.

2 Where possible, use natural features such as rock pools to trap fish.

3 Once in, the fish may be netted or speared.

Fish and Wild Fowl Snares Snaring fish is not as easy as snaring small game, but it works on similar principles and can be achieved with time, care and observation. Take a normal animal snare and attach it to the end of a stick, which should be at least 200cm (80ins) long. Tie an extension on to the end of the snare wire so that you can close the noose at will. (see page 99.)

Fishing Nets It may even be possible for the survivor to make and use his own fishing net – a gill net – as long as he has enough line (a possible source for this would be a parachute rigging line). First decide how long the net has to be, and then tie the top line of the net between two saplings or stakes the right distance apart. Tie another line below this to define the width of the net. Any nylon lines that are available should have their inner cores stripped out. Take a piece of this inner core and double it. Tie it to the upper of the two lines using an overhand loop. The two ends, which should be 30% longer than the required width of the net, should then be allowed to hang down loose. It is now just a matter of repetitive knotting; but you probably have lots of time on your hands. Depending on your location, the materials available and your ability to manage it, make your net as large as possible.

Providing a stream is not too wide nets can be erected right across it; if it is, then the stream can often be dammed to make it narrower. Support the net by stretching a line across and secure the bottom edge in the water with heavy stones. In a larger body of water, such as a river, nets should be set just above or below an eddy.

Wherever they are set, it should always be in a stretch of quiet water. On a lake shore the net should be set at right angles to the bank, preferably off a small headland.

Making a Fish Net

1 Place your top line between two trees and hitch a double length of cord every 3cm.

2 Cross tie the hanging strands with a simple granny knot to form a diamond pattern.

Providing you have the materials, making a fish net is always a good idea. Not only can it be used for catching fish and game, it is also handy when gathering plants.

Minnow Traps Small fish such as minnows can be found in most water, especially where it is shallow, such as at the edge of a river or a lake. A normal net will be too large, but several fine-meshed nets can be constructed from a pair of women's tights. Cut a length off the tights, knotting one end if it is not the toe piece; splay the open end around a ring of stiff wire, and secure this to a forked branch. A well-perforated tin can attached in the same way will serve the same task. Do not disregard the food value of very small fish; dried and roasted in quantity, they make good eating.

Eel Traps A simple eel trap can be made from a suitable box. On each side of the box, near the top, make a couple of small holes. Inside the box lay some ripe meat as bait. Weight the box and put it into the water, checking it every two or three days. (To do this, take the box out of the water first and part-empty it before opening it to see what you have caught. Eels are proverbially slippery, and it is almost impossible to hold on to them long enough to lift them out of the water.)

Spearing Spearing fish can be difficult, especially in the hours of daylight, but with practice it is possible. The fish will need to be

Spear Fishing

• Stand directly above a 'run' used by fish.

• Use a strong, three-pointed spear.

• Don't throw it – stab directly downwards.

• Chase any wounded fish.

Tickling a Trout

When you get near what looks like a good spot for trout, lie on the bank and dip your hand in the water to bring it to water temperature. Begin at the downstream end of any possible cover, working upstream, gently and carefully feeling for fish. If fish are present you will encounter the tail first. This should be gently stroked a few times before moving the strokes up the body towards the gills. Once your hand is under the gills, flick the fish quickly out of the water and on to the bank.

There are three main factors to tickling trout successfully:

• Knowing where the fish can be found. Carefully study the water, and discover where they hide.

• Be relaxed. Most people will flinch at the first contact with a slimy fish – prepare yourself mentally not to react. Move slowly and gently, and touch it lightly.

• Be warned that trout are very slippery fish to handle – roll your body back on to the bank as you flick the fish out of the water.

fairly plentiful if you use a single-point spear, and you are advised to use a three-pronged head or trident for greater efficiency. The spear should be stabbed into the water at the fish, not thrown; and the stab should be aimed directly downwards. Spearing in this way reduces refraction in the water, and thus the risk of misjudging the angle; and will also pin any speared fish to the streambed. The best position for this method is standing directly over a fish run. Make sure the spear is strong enough to withstand the thrashing of a large fish. Always chase after a badly wounded fish, as they will not go far.

In much the same way, fish can be shot using a bow and arrow. Use long arrows which will be visible above the surface and will restrict the movement of any wounded fish trying to escape.

Tickling Trout Trout are extremely nervous fish which are to be found only in clear, moving water. They prefer to conceal themselves beneath some sort of cover such as undercut banks, rocks and logs, or even in water rat holes. When they are in this cover it is possible to catch one by hand, something which would be impossible in open water.

Killing or Stunning with Poison Poisons, usually derived from plant sources, are used by some native peoples to catch fish. Fish are quickly affected by poison being introduced into the water, normally rising to the surface quite soon. The speed at which the poison works will depend on the water temperature. Around 21 degrees C (70 degrees F) or warmer is ideal.

One of the most common poisons is rotenone, a substance found in tropical plants that stuns or kills cold-blooded animals while leaving the flesh safe to eat. The following plants can be used to stun or kill fish:

- **Derris eliptica** is the main source of commercially produced rotenone, which is a natural pesticide. The roots from this large order of tropical shrubs and woody vines are ground and mixed with water, which is then thrown into the river. Where possible the mixture is best left overnight to strengthen.
- **Anamirta cocculus** is a woody vine which grows in southern Asia and on islands in the South Pacific. Crush the bean-shaped seeds and throw them in the water.
- **Croton tiglium** is a shrub or small tree that grows in waste areas on islands of the South Pacific and which produces seed capsules. Crush the seeds and throw them into the water.
- **Barringtonia** is a large tree that grows near the sea in Malaysia and other tropical regions. It produces a fleshy one-seeded fruit that can often be found rotting on the ground. Both the seeds and the bark of this tree can be used as fish poison by crushing and throwing into the water.
- On the coastline, burning coral or seashells can produce lime. The white dust residue can be thrown into the water.

Crustaceans Crustaceans include crabs, lobsters, crayfish, shrimp and prawns. All are edible, and can be found in fresh and salt water around the world. Most are best caught at night, using a light such as a torch held near the surface of the water. Mussels, limpets, clams and periwinkles can also be eaten, as can scallops, sea urchins and starfish. To clean a crustacean, throw away the intestines and gills – the rest of the meat, including that inside the shell and claws, can be eaten. Warning: All crustaceans must be thoroughly cooked as soon as they are caught, as they do not keep. If you delay in eating any crustacean or you fail to cook it properly, then you run the risk of the worst type of food poisoning.

Frogs Small amphibians such as newts and frogs can also provide a good meal. They are to be found around fresh water, usually revealing their presence by croaking. However, any croaking will stop as you approach, so have plenty of patience and keep still until they are fooled into thinking that you have gone away again. During the mating season (February/March) catching frogs becomes quite easy. All you need to do is to splash the back of your hand gently against the surface water and frogs will jump onto it. It is possible to catch several in as many minutes.

Preparing Fish, Snakes and Amphibians Once you have caught a fish you will need to bleed it immediately. To gut the fish, slit open its stomach from

Fishing hints

- Approach the fishing water making as little noise and vibration as you can.

- Don't let your shadow fall on the water.

- Make no sudden movements or noises.

- Try to spot the fishes' natural prey in that water, and bait with it.

- Spread ground bait.

- Cast up-stream and let your bait float down to the fish.

Cleaning Fish

• As soon as you land a fish, kill it by hitting the head with a stone or club.

• Slit the stomach from jaw to tail.

• Scrape out the innards.

• Wash out the body cavity thoroughly.

• Hold the tail and scrape off the scales, moving down towards the head.

• Unless you are going to cook on a spit, cut off the head.

• Don't eat fish raw – cook by spit-roasting, baking in embers, or frying.

• Keep head, tail and guts for bait.

Crustaceans

• All crabs, crayfish, shrimps, prawns, etc, start to spoil the moment they are caught.

• Cook them at once, by dropping them alive into boiling water.

• Only thorough cooking destroys any organisms they may contain.

• Throw away the innards and the gills.

• The meat inside the shell and claws is edible.

• Failure to cook quickly enough, or thoroughly, invites serious food poisoning.

Gutting and cleaning fish before cooking; split open the stomach (top), scrape out the inside (middle), and clean thoroughly in fresh water.

the lower jaw to the tail and scrape out the innards. Wash the area thoroughly to flush out any remaining pieces. Fish can be cooked with their scales on, but if you have the time they make more pleasant eating with their scales removed. To do this, scrape downwards with a knife from the tail to the head. Fish such as catfish and sturgeon, which do not have any scales, can be skinned instead. Smaller fish, e.g. those less than 3 inches long, do not need gutting, but some will still need scaling or skinning. The head should also be cut off unless you are going to cook the fish on a spit. Raw fish may contain parasites, and should only be eaten cold if the means to cook are outside your capabilities. This should very seldom be the case if you have a fire; fish can be cooked in a wide variety of ways – spit-roasted, baked, boiled or fried. Fish heads, tails and intestines all make good bait.

Snakes and Reptiles Skin a snake by cutting off its head and slitting its body skin from the severed end downwards for about 20cm (8 inches). Peel back the skin to the length of the cut; grip the flesh and continue pulling the skin downward until within a few centimetres of the tail; then cut off the remainder. If the snake body looks bloated or lumpy, split it open and remove the innards. Cut the body flesh into small sections and cook – roasting or boiling is best. Lizards, frogs and turtles are good to eat. Before cooking, take off the head and skin; this is particularly important in the case of frogs, as their skins may contain a poison. Turtles will need to be boiled first to remove the shell. The turtle meat can then be sliced up and used to make a tasty soup with vegetables.

Molluscs Shellfish make an excellent base for a soup to which vegetables can be added. In addition, they can be boiled, steamed or baked in their shells.

Methods of Cooking

The proper preparation and cooking of food will make it safer to eat as well as more appetizing and digestible.

If possible you must try to have one hot meal a day. Most foods, whether animal or plant, require some form of preparation, whether washing, cleaning, scaling, plucking or skinning. How you cook the food also makes a difference, and will eliminate wastage. In the event of a food surplus the survivor is advised to prolong its edible life by preserving.

Roasting Stick Initial roasting should be done over a high heat, which will crust the outside of the meat and seal the juices in. This is followed by slowly turning the meat over a more placid flame. The dripping juices will cause the flames to flare and burn the meat; prevent this by placing a tray below the roast. These juices can be used to baste the roast, and improve its flavour. Larger animals (those larger than a domestic cat) should be cut into small

A roasting stick.

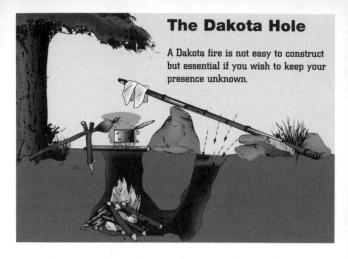

The Dakota Hole

A Dakota fire is not easy to construct but essential if you wish to keep your presence unknown.

pieces before roasting. These can be roasted by simply pushing the meat onto a stick and holding it over or near hot embers. If you do not want to sit and hold the stick you could construct an arm or a crane.

Automatic Spit With a little ingenuity you can prevent food from burning by constructing a spit which is turned by the wind. This not only cooks the food evenly, but saves the time which is otherwise wasted while watching to make sure the food does not burn. A normal crane is fitted with a wire line (cord will burn through) on which the meat is hung. Adding a flat slab of bark about the size of your open hand will allow the wind to twist the meat; a natural counter-action will turn it back the other way.

Boiling Tough meat will need to be boiled to tenderize it, even if you intend to finish it off by some other cooking method. Any nutritional value leached out of the meat through the cooking process will also be retained in the water, which makes boiling a very efficient cooking method as long as you retain and use the water. One thing to remember, however, is that the higher in altitude you go, the longer it will take for water to reach boiling point due to the reduction in air pressure. Above 4000m (12,000ft) cooking raw food by boiling becomes almost impossible and should not be attempted.

Water can be boiled even if you have no metal container – you just have to look for alternatives. Suitable containers, which will not burn while the water is boiling, include half a green coconut; or a short length of bamboo, cut just below each of two joints; or a suitable large shell. A large single banana leaf, or a water-proof container made from a piece of folded birch bark, will also hold water while it is boiled as long as the fire is kept low and the leaf or bark kept moist. Use thorns to pin the folded corner points.

Baking Baking is a less intense form of cooking than roasting, and the heat is more constant. To be baked food must be enclosed, either in an oven, or in a wrapping of leaves or clay in a pit under the fire, or in any closed container. Baking is best done with glowing coals rather than flame.

Steaming Steaming food can be done without having a container. It is best for foods which do not need much cooking, such as tender greens. The other advantage of steaming is that it retains more of the nutrients in the food than any other method of cooking. To use this method, first dig a pit and place in it a layer of heated stones. Cover the stones with leaves and put the food to be cooked on top of the leaves. Use more leaves to cover over the food, and push a stick down into the food space. Finally, pack a top layer of earth over the leaves and around the stick. Withdrawing the stick will leave a little hole that leads down to the food space.

When water is poured down this hole it will hit the hot rocks and turn to steam, slowly but effectively cooking your food.

Hangi The hangi is a cooking method which originally came from Polynesia. It is slow and safe, especially if you need to be away from camp, or if you have no utensils to cook your food in. First, dig a pit five times the size of the food parcel it must accommodate. Lay your tinder and kindling in the middle of the pit. Make a pyramid fire above the hole, placing each layer of logs at right angles to the last layer. Build this up to a height of about six layers, with fist-sized stones and rocks placed between the layers. (Do not use soft, porous or flaking stones such as limestone, as these may explode when exposed to heat.) Once the fire is established it will burn its way through the log pyramid and the hot stones will fall into the pit.

Rake the hot embers to the side of the pit exposing the hot stones. The food should be wrapped in large, clean leaves (make sure that they are not poisonous) and placed on the stones. Meat and any other food which needs the most cooking should be placed at the hottest point of the pit, that is, the centre. Softer foods such as vegetables should be placed nearer the edges. Once all the food has been packed into the hangi, cover the pit with a roof of foliage and seal it with the earth spoil, to keep the heat in and prevent animals from foraging. The food may take

The Hangi

❶ Pyramid fire with stones throughout.

❷ Fire pit five times larger than food parcels.

❸ Covering of foliage and fresh earth.

❹ Food parcels wrapped in large leaves.

A well-prepared hangi will cook your food while you are away from camp.

three to four hours to cook in this way, but the advantage is that it will not become overcooked even if left for up to eight hours.

Improvised Haybox Another method of slow-cooking food is to construct an improvised haybox. This will prove especially valuable where firewood is scarce, and allows for a meal to cook safely while you are out foraging or attending to more pressing matters. Another benefit of the haybox is that it cooks food well and cannot overcook or burn it.

A box or container is lined with a thick layer of insulating material; if no such container is available then a polythene bag will do. As the name implies, hay was used as the insulating material but more modern insulating materials such as polystyrene or crumpled newspaper can also be used. The other requirement is a can which will act as a cooking pot, preferably one with a well-fitting lid. Heat your meal over a fire until it starts to boil, then seal the cooking pot with a tight-fitting lid. Place it at the centre of your haybox and surround it with well-packed insulating material. Leave for approximately five hours before opening. It is advisable (although not necessary) to bring the pot back to the boil over an open fire before eating.

Food Preservation

Food-gathering may not always be successful: there will be times when game will be difficult to find or catch, or when the weather will make food collection difficult. The survivor must not rely on the assumption that a regular supply of wild food will always be available. In these circumstances, knowing how to preserve and store foods is a valid survival skill. Preserved food will not only back up fresh supplies but may also be carried with you if you plan to move on.

The aim of food preservation is to prevent the deterioration of the food and so prevent wastage. A cold climate makes food preservation relatively easy, as the food can be quickly frozen. To do this, cut it into small strips or pieces and lay it out on the ground around the shelter. Make sure that scavengers do not steal it while it is freezing. Frozen food should also be stored at least 6ft above ground level, out of the reach of other hungry animals.

Meat can be dried either in the sun and wind or else over a fire. The aim of drying is to drive as much of the moisture content from the meat as possible. This not only concentrates its nutritional value, but will also preserve it longer from decomposition and moulds. A piece of dried meat should contain only about 5% of its pre-dried content of moisture. Meat should be cut into long, thin strips and placed to dry on a platform safe from scavengers but open to the sun and wind. The process may take up to two weeks, and during this time the strips need to be kept dry from any rain and free from flies.

In warm or damp weather when meat deteriorates rapidly, smoking over a low fire can save it from spoiling for some time. Care must be taken to keep the meat from getting too hot. Cutting it across the grain into thin strips and either drying it in the wind or smokng it will produce 'jerky', which was one of the staple foods of the pioneers. Fish should be flattened by removing the backbone, and skewered in that position for smoking; thin willow

Air dried meat.

• When you have more meat than you can eat in a day or two, preserve it for leaner times or for travelling.

• If near the seashore, boil and distil seawater to extract salt. Rub salt into meat and air-dry it; or store in a salt-heavy brine solution.

• If inland, in a hot climate, slice meat thinly and dry in the sun.

• If the sunlight is inadequate, smoke thin slices slowly over a fire.

• In a cold climate, cut meat into small strips and freeze it.

branches with the bark removed make good skewers. Willow, alder, cottonwood, birch, and dwarf birch make the best smoking woods, and are found throughout the Arctic and sub-Arctic regions. Pitch woods such as fir and pine should not be used.

A small version of a North American tepee with a platform constructed in the middle makes an excellent smokehouse. By tying meat to the upper ends of the poles and closing the smoke flaps a good concentration of smoke is obtained. Try to create a fire with little flame which produces quantities of smoke. The meat will be ready when it is brittle.

Plants, leaves and fruits can also be dried by the methods described. To dry fruits successfully, cut them into thin slices first. Mushrooms also dry well, but may need to be soaked in water before use. Berries are best preserved by being turned into jam or jelly.

Salt Brine Salt is difficult to find in the wild, but if you are near the coast it is well worth your while simply boiling seawater until it evaporates. Salt can be used in the preservation of either wet or dry food.

In cool climates, joint your game into usable pieces, rub with salt and allow to hang in the fresh air; repeat the salt-rubbing process for several days. If a container is available, make a strong slurry of salt and water (natural sea water is not strong enough for preservation); submerge your meat completely in this, and cover. Store the container in a cool, shaded spot.

There are several ways one can navigate and define direction in a survival situation, from using the sun, moon and stars to employing the modern satellite Global Positioning System (GPS) to fix your position.

To the survivor any method of navigation is acceptable providing it is accurate, but a sound knowledge of how to use a map and compass will always prove a bonus. Other basic navigational skills, not dependent on map, compass or GPS, can also be learnt and are extremely useful in survival situations.

Maps A map is a sheet of paper on which an aerial view of the area it represents is drawn. The detail included on the map will vary, depending on who did the survey, what use the map is intended for, and the scale.

Most maps have one thing in common: almost all have a grid overlay dividing the map into squares which are either lettered, numbered or both. Most maps also contain a legend explaining the scale, distance and symbolized features.

Different maps are made to suit different purposes. Aircraft operators and strategic planners normally use maps with a scale of 1/250,000; these provide only generalized information and show only principal features. Maps used by the military for route selection are normally to a scale of 1/50,000; these show detailed features and relief. This book uses a 1/50,000 scale map to illustrate the meaning of elevation, contour intervals, conventional signs, the grid system, and information on magnetic variation.

Compasses A compass is a precision instrument which allows the user to identify North and thus the other cardinal points. Used in conjunction with a map, it allows for navigation over the surface of the planet. There are many shapes and sizes of compass, but all work on the principle of a magnetized needle continually pointing North. Always remember that any compass works on the magnetic attraction situated close to the North Pole; local power supplies or heavy metal objects can pull the needle from its correct course. Most compass manufacturers dampen the movement of the needle by filling the compass housing with a liquid. This

LIFESAVER
The Compass

This compass is constructed with a clear plastic base and a compass housing which contains the magnetic needle. The base of the compass has a magnifying glass and is etched with a variety of scales and a number of romers – scales to accurately divide a grid square into tenths to help calculate grid references. The rim of the compass housing can be rotated, and is marked with segments showing degrees, mills or both, while printed on the base is an arrow and orienteering lines.

The 'bearing' gives the direction to a certain point. It can be defined as the number of degrees in an angle measured clockwise from a fixed northern gridline ('easting'). The bearing for North is always 0/360 (the number of degrees in a circle) or 0/6400 (the number of mills in a full circle).

Map Scale

Maps to a scale of 1/50,000 show all roads, tracks, paths, rivers, streams, lakes and most man-made features. In addition they indicate ground relief using contour lines, and areas of forest. The numbered grid divides the map into 1000m (1,093 yard) squares that convert into longitude and latitude bearings.

Finding Your Way

• Given a rough idea of your position relative to inhabited areas, you can find and follow an approximate direction across country even if you are a lifelong city-dweller.

• Map, compass, and basic knowledge of their use are very valuable; but even without them you need not be 'lost'.

• You may have the means to make yourself a simple compass.

• Even if not, the sun by day and the stars by night will always show you the direction of North.

sometimes produces a bubble, but providing that this is not large it should not affect the operation of the compass. This book uses a 'Silva'-type compass to illustrate the various uses, and its relationship to a map.

Conventional Signs Every map has a panel of conventional signs which indicate a variety of objects such as roads, railways, rivers, cliffs, buildings, etc. In a survival situation identifying a man-made object on a map which covers your area can lead you to safety. A complete study should be done of any map in your possession to establish not only your position, but also what else is in the area. Even if it is barren of any human structures it may guide you to a more habitable place of food and shelter.

Contours Contours are used to represent different elevations – e.g. valleys, hills and mountains – on a flat surface such as a paper map. They are intended to give a perspective view of shape and elevation. Each contour line follows the same height around the hills, into the re-entrants, and over the spurs. On the 1/50,000 Ordnance Survey map the contour lines are 50 feet apart. Therefore, if the lines are close together it follows that the land is rising very quickly, and if far apart, that the slope is gentle. Contour values, which are given to the nearest metre, are marked so that they read facing uphill. Remember, however, that while the heights are in metres, the contour lines are 50 feet apart.

Setting a Map by Inspection If you possess a map that you know to represent the local area, you will be able to orientate yourself. Look for an obvious and permanent landmark, for example a river, road or mountain. Identify the feature on the map, and then simply align the map to the landmark. The map is now 'set' to conform to the surrounding features. If you do not have a compass, make a note of a distant feature at one of the cardinal points – North, East, West or South.

Setting a Map by Compass You can set any scale map and align it with the surrounding terrain by simply using a compass.

Reading Contours

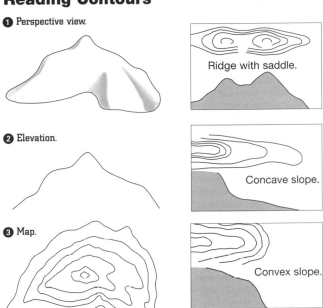

1 Perspective view.

Ridge with saddle.

2 Elevation.

Concave slope.

3 Map.

Convex slope.

Choose a North-South grid line on the map, and lay a flat edge of the compass along it with the direction arrow pointing towards North (top of the map). Then, holding the map and compass together, turn both until the compass needle points North. The map is now set to conform to the surrounding features.

Finding a Grid Reference Almost all maps are covered with light horizontal and vertical lines, each marked with a two-digit number. These are called grid lines – on a 1/50,000 map they are blue and spaced 1km (0.62 miles) apart. The vertical lines are called 'eastings': these are always given first when quoting a grid reference. The horizontal lines are called 'northings'; these are given after the eastings. The numbers straddling the left grid line of the easting and the centre bottom of the northing defines each grid square – an example is illustrated on page 132.

As each grid square measures 1000m by 1000m – which is quite a large area – it is desirable to reduce this by calculating a six-figure grid reference. This is done by mentally dividing the square into tenths – e.g. halfway up or across a square would be '5'. This reference is then added after the relevant easting or northing figure. To gauge the tenths accurately use the romer on the compass, or a protractor as illustrated.

Taking a Compass Bearing from the Map Once you have established where you are, and where you wish to go, you can work out your route. Plot the most logical route to your objective, taking into account the distance, terrain and any obstacles. Divide your route up into 'legs', if possible finishing each leg close to a prominent feature, e.g. a bend in a river or the corner of

Grid Reference

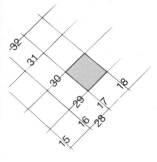

A compass with a built in romer makes it easy to subdivide a grid square and produce a more accurate six figure reference.

The example shown is 17528

a forest area. If using a 1/50,000 scale map the ideal distance for each leg should not be longer than the length of your compass base.

First take a bearing from where you are (call this point A) to the feature at the end of your first leg (call this point B). Place one edge of the compass along the line joining A to B, making sure that the direction-of-travel arrow is pointing in the way you want to go. Hold the compass plate firmly in position and rotate the compass dial so that the lines engraved in the dial base are parallel to the North-South grid lines on the map.

Finally, read off the bearing next to the line-of-march arrow on the compass housing. To walk on this bearing, simply keep the magnetic arrow pointing North over the etched arrow in the base, and follow the line-of-march arrow as illustrated. Repeat this process for each leg.

Magnetic Variation When we talk about 'North', bear in mind that there are three Norths. True North is not generally used in navigation; it is the fixed location of the North Pole. Grid North is more familiar – it is the North indicated by the gridlines on a map. Magnetic North is where the needle on the compass always points due to the strong magnetic attraction generated by the Earth's magnetic field. However, the direction of magnetic North may vary by a small fraction from year to year due to changes in this magnetic field. This difference can be calculated using the information shown on the map, i.e. the date it was printed and the degree of variation. This variation is then either added or subtracted to Grid North to get a more accurate bearing. Put simply: 'Mag to Grid, get rid' – i.e. subtract the variation from your compass bearing before applying it to the map. 'Grid to Mag, add' – i.e. add the variation to your map bearing before applying it to your compass.

Keeping on Course Three factors will determine which route you take: the weather, the time of day, and the terrain between you and your final destination. In good visibility, select features that are both prominent on your map and visible to the eye. Once you have taken a bearing, choose a feature along the line of march and head towards it. This saves you constantly looking at your compass. A back bearing will help keep you on course if the terrain pushes you off track, i.e. you are forced to avoid some obstacle.

Mistakes in poor visibility can be avoided if you consult the map every time you meet a prominent feature. Careful study of the map should provide you with a mental picture of the ground relief, which will in turn warn you of any obstacles such as rivers or marshland.

There is a tendency during conditions of fog or poor visibility to wander downhill when you are contouring. Every 100m or so take a few steps uphill to compensate for this. Don't forget that you will move slower in poor visibility.

Global Positioning System (GPS)
Developed by the United States Department of Defense, the GPS system consists of 24 military satellites which orbit the Earth, continually giving out the time and their position. Receiver units on Earth pick up this information and use it to determine location. Designed for the military, the system now guides most of the world's shipping, aircraft (and 'smart' missiles).

Many outdoor workers and enthusiasts also carry hand-held units, no larger than a mobile phone. Receiving units commercially available to civilians vary, as does their accuracy. A deliberate error, called Selective Availability (SA), was built into the system. This 'dithers' the signals so that only a Coarse Acquisition (CA) can be obtained, therefore reducing accuracy to about 40m (130 feet). The SA can be overridden for military use by a 'P' code, and this gives an accuracy of about 10m (33 feet).

Magnetic Variation: Don't Panic!

Some people put a lot of emphasis on adding or subtracting the magnetic variation, but for survival purposes you can virtually forget about it. By simply shortening the legs of your selected route and choosing a prominent feature to march towards or from, you reduce the risk of magnetic variation error. Some will criticize me for saying this; but I have never bothered to work out the magnetic variation when walking – and I have walked across more desert, jungle and Arctic tundra than most. That said, it is advisable to adjust the variation when plotting long routes across barren land, or when travelling by vehicle.

LIFESAVER
GPS Limitations

The GPS requires tuition in its proper use, and is not a compass in the normal sense. Despite its excellent qualities, the GPS system can be shut down at times. In addition, the units have a high battery drain. Do not become complacent – don't forget your compass.

How it Works The GPS receiver searches for and locks on to satellite signals. The more signals you receive, the greater the accuracy, but a minimum of four is required. The information received is then collated into a usable form – for example, a grid reference, height above sea level, or a longitude and latitude.

By measuring your position in relation to the satellites, the receiver is able to calculate your position. This is called satellite ranging. It is also able to update your position, speed and track while you are on the move; and can pinpoint future waypoints, thereby taking away the need to find recognizable landmarks.

GPS

❶ Hand held unit locks on to any satellite in its range.

❷ At least four satellites need to be available. The more contacts, the more accurate will be the information returned.

❸ Satellites return signal to GPS unit.

❹ The unit translates the signal into information required; grid reference; height above sea level etc.

Making a Sketch Map

All aircraft and most vehicles which venture away from civilization carry maps, and these should be located before attempting to improvise a sketch map. If you are left with no option, the sketch map will help you to plan any travel, indicate to others the route taken, and provide an easy reference to navigation.

A sketch map is best drawn similar in orientation to that of a normal map, i.e. with North at the top centre of your sketch. Choose a high vantage point to observe the surrounding countryside, and fill in the detail working outwards from the centre. Divide your map using a distance grid ruled along the top and down the left side. Next draw in all prominent features – mountains, rivers, forests, marshes, etc – using the grid as an estimate of distance. If no coloured pens are available, black and white line drawings are fine; information can be qualified by the addition of notes. Mark camp sites and routes as you travel.

Electronic Compass Electronic compasses have been around for a number of years, but until recently they have not behaved well and were fairly unreliable. An improved generation has started to appear which provides something between a magnetic compass and GPS. The electronic compass has a number of features well suited to the survival situation. These include course memory, night vision back-light, automatic route reverse, stored bearings, and a clock which gives time and distance. Electronic compasses are simple to operate, and are extremely handy during the hours of darkness. Power is a consideration, as the unit runs on batteries; however, the battery life is around 200 hours and most are fitted with automatic shut-down.

Improvised Compass By magnetizing a small, straight piece of metal such as a needle, pin or razor blade, and suspending it so

Back Bearing

If you become disorientated there is a simple way to pinpoint your position and keep yourself on course. This is called a back bearing; as the name implies, it is the opposite to a forward (normal) bearing. For example, if a bearing is 260°, and you subtract half a circle – 180° – you get a back bearing of 80°. If the original bearing is less than 180° you simply add 180°; e.g. if your bearing is 60°, plus 180° gives you a back bearing of 240°.

This has several uses. If you leave a prominent feature and move across rough terrain which forces you off your line of march, you can always double-check by converting your bearing to a back bearing and re- fixing on the feature behind you.

By converting the bearing of two landmarks that you can identify on the map, it is possible to establish your correct position. Take a bearing to the first landmark; e.g. say this is 280°. If you wish, calculate the magnetic variation, which we will say is 5°, and subtract. This leaves us with a revised bearing of 275°. Since this is greater than 180°, a back bearing can be achieved by subtraction of that number, i.e. giving us 95°.

This bearing is applied to the compass dial and the edge of the base is set against the landmark shown on the map. Pivot the whole compass until the orienteering lines in the base of the housing are running parallel to the eastings. This should allow you to draw a line from the feature at an angle of 95°.

Repeat the whole procedure for your second landmark, and draw another line. Your position is indicated where the two lines cross.

that it can swing freely, it is possible to make a simple compass. The piece of metal can be magnetized by stroking it in one direction with one pole of a magnet. Magnets can be found in any radio set, installed as part of the speaker. The pointer will then need to be suspended – with a small object such as a needle or razor blade this can be done by floating it on water.

To do this, improvise by sticking the pointer through a small piece of cork, or by balancing it on three matchsticks or a small twig. Warning: Remember that the container which holds the water must not be made of metal, as this may affect the magnetic field and cause the pointer to give a false reading. Also, remember that after a time the magnetizing effect on the pointer will wear off and will have to be repeated.

Steel pointers can also be magnetized with electricity. For this you will need a battery that is capable of producing more than 6 volts, and a good length of insulated copper wire. Suitable wire may be found in the coils inside radios and generators, or any electrical equipment in most kinds of vehicles. To magnetize the pointer, wrap the wire around it as many times as you can. Strip the ends of the wire of any insulation, and attach to the battery for 15-30 minutes. Ensure that the wire wrapped around the pointer is long enough or it will get too hot. If this happens, disconnect from the battery and allow them to cool before starting again. Once the pointer has been magnetized (this may take several attempts), the end indicating North will be that nearer to the negative battery terminal (remember: N stands for both Negative and North).

Finding Direction Without a Compass

Compasses and GPS systems may be the easiest and most convenient methods of finding a direction, but survival starts in the most unusual places, and the odds are you will be without either. Luckily the most important aspect of survival navigation is direction, and this can be established through a number of time-honoured methods by using a bit of intelligence.

Stick and Stone Method The accuracy of this method depends on using level ground and marking the shadow with some degree of accuracy. A North/South indicator can be produced if a line is drawn at right angles to your East/West line; any other direction is simply a calculation from these cardinal points.

- On a sunny day, find or cut a stick about one metre (39ins) long, and push it upright into some level ground.
- The stick will cast a shadow. Using a small stone, mark the end of the shadow as accurately as possible.
- After 15 to 20 minutes the shadow will have moved. Using a second stone, mark the tip of the new shadow.
- On the earth, draw a straight line running through the positions of both stones. This is your East/West line.
- Put your left foot close to the first stone, and your right foot close to the second. You are now facing North.

Using a Watch Using an analogue watch face allows us to find direction. In the Northern Hemisphere this is achieved by the following method. Check that your watch is accurately set to local time, reset for any local summer time which may have been added.

- Point the hour hand at the sun.
- Using a thin twig, cast a shadow along the hour hand through the central pivot.
- Bisect the angle between the hour hand and 12 o'clock.
- This line will be pointing due South, North being furthest from the sun.

The same procedure applies in the Southern Hemisphere, once again having set your watch to local time:

- Point the number 12 at the sun.
- Using a thin twig, cast a shadow to achieve more accuracy.
- Bisect the angle between the hour hand and 12 o'clock.
- The end of this line nearest to the sun indicates North.

Stick and Stone Method

❶ Put a stick vertically in the ground.

❷ Mark the end of its shadow with a stone.

❸ After 20 minutes mark the end of the shadow with your second stone.

❹ Your two stones lie east-to-west.

❺ North is perpendicular to a line drawn between the stones.

Place your LEFT foot next to the FIRST stone and your RIGHT next to the SECOND stone to face North.

N

Navigation by Night

Navigation by the stars has been practised for thousands of years, and having learnt about the stars is hugely beneficial in survival navigation. Bright stars that seem to be grouped together in a pattern are called constellations. The shapes of these constellations and their relationships to each other do not alter. Because of the Earth's rotation, the whole of the night sky appears to revolve around one central point; and this can help you to find directions.

The North Star In the Northern Hemisphere a faint star called Polaris, the Pole or North Star, marks the central point. Because of its position it always appears to remain in the same place – above the North Pole.

As long as Polaris can be seen the direction of True North can be found. To find Polaris, first locate the constellation variously known as 'The Great Bear', 'The Plough' or 'The Big Dipper'. A

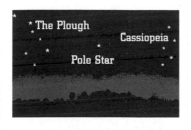

line through the two stars furthest from the 'handle' always points towards Polaris. Take the distance between the two stars and then follow the line straight for about six times the distance. At this point you will see the Pole Star. If you are unsure which way to look or wish to confirm that you have found Polaris, look for another constellation called Cassiopeia. The five stars which make up this constellation are patterned in the shape of a slightly flattened 'W'. Cassiopeia is positioned almost opposite the Plough, and Polaris can be found midway between them. As long as the sky is clear the Plough,

Cassiopeia and Polaris remain visible all night when seen from any country north of 40 degrees N latitude.

The Southern Hemisphere The Southern Hemisphere does not have a version of Polaris conveniently marking the direction of South. Instead you will need to locate the constellation of the Southern Cross, made up of four main stars with a fainter fifth one just off the centre point of the cross. Take a line through the longer of the cross's arms and extend it for four and a half times its length. If you have the right line, it should pass through a group of four very faint stars shortly after the Cross. This will take you to the point where you will find South. To make navigation easier, find a land-mark directly below this point to indicate South in a terrestrial plane.

Star Movement Method Clear skies cannot always be guaran-teed, but if there is only partial obstruction by cloud and you are still able to see individual constellations, navigation by the stars can still be employed. The Star Movement Method is based on knowing how the stars wheel around the sky. Depending on which way they are moving, you should be able to get a rough indication of the direction you are facing. To do this you will need two fixed reference points, such as two sticks set in the ground like the sights of a gun. These should be aimed at any prominent star.

Star Movement

If the star moves right, you are facing South; left=North; down=West; up=East

If the star appears to be:

- Looping flatly towards the right, you are fac-ing approximately South.
- Looping flatly towards the left, you are facing approximate-ly North.
- Rising, you are facing approximately East.
- Descending, you are facing approximately West.

You can also use your eye as the second fixed reference point, as long as your head is steadied against some solid object first. With this method, it is best to use a series of glances to observe the star. Fixed staring will produce an optical illusion of either the star wandering about, or not moving at all.

The Moon

The movement of the moon also follows a set pattern and can aid navigation. There are two methods which can be used:

The Quarter Moons Both waxing and waning quarter moons can be used. Draw a line through the horns down to the horizon. The point where it touches gives a rough indication of South, if you are in the Northern Hemisphere, and North if you are in the Southern Hemisphere. Although not very accurate this will at least provide you with a rough guide while travelling at night.

The Moon and Time Make sure that your watch is correct and set to local time. The phases of the moon pass through certain directions at certain times; so by using a watch in conjunction with the table below you should be able to get a good idea of the direction you are travelling in.

	1ST QUARTER	FULL MOON	LAST QUARTER
1800	South	East	
2100	Southwest	Southeast	
Midnight	West	South	East
0300	Southwest	Southeast	
0600	West	South	

Vegetation Tips to Navigation

Using vegetation to find your direction is not very accurate, but can give you an idea of your heading. Trees and shrubs which are perennial tend to produce more foliage on the side most exposed to the sun, that is the side nearest to the Equator, and the more slender types of trees such as willows, poplars and alders have a tendency to lean towards the sun.

Strong prevailing winds may also cause a greater amount of foliage to grow on the leeward side. Use common sense and observation to discern whether wind or sun has had greater effect. Moss prefers the damp and the shade, tending to grow on the side of a tree or rock that is least exposed to the sun – i.e. they tend to grow facing towards the Poles rather than the Equator.

Prevailing Winds

Prevailing winds may not blow all the time, especially in the interiors of large land masses. Sometimes local winds will hold sway. For a wind to be prevailing, it must remain constant for a few days at a time. In the desert, they will dictate the shape of the sand dunes. As long as you know which way the prevailing wind blows, the shape of the dunes will give you a rudimentary idea of direction.

Winds around coastal areas and mountains are also apt to have their own patterns. During the morning they tend to blow offshore and in the evening they change direction and blow onshore.

The choice of whether to travel or to stay put is one of the great dilemmas any survivor must face. Without communications it is difficult to assess whether there will even be a rescue attempt, let alone how successful searchers may be in locating you.

The factors governing any decision should be based on where you are, your chances of survival if you stay there, where you intend moving to, and the related hazards in getting there.

A realistic judgement of your physical, mental and material resources – your ability to travel and to reach a given point accurately – must also be made.

Once you have determined the need to travel you must prepare. Before you start, it is important to check the weather and work out a travel routine based on the type of terrain and conditions you will be passing through.

The pace should be steady and unrushed, with a break of five to ten minutes at least every hour. Use this break productively, not just to rest but also to evaluate your progress so far and to consider the next part of your route. This is also the time for minor repairs and adjustments to clothing and kit. Make sure that you do not go beyond your physical limits – and take into consideration that your feet will be doing most of the work while you are travelling. It is wise to take care of them; prevention is much better than cure. At the end of every day's march remove all footwear and wash your feet; also wash and clean your socks, stockings or footrags, and boots or shoes. Make a fire and dry the footwear overnight; that way it will be clean and dry for you to put on again the next morning.

Travel Equipment

1 Wrap your kit in a blanket or tarpaulin and carry it over your shoulder.

2 Alternatively, if the materials are available, make a pack to carry your kit on your back.

LIFESAVER
Obstacles

Where survival travel is concerned, obstacles can be divided into two types: natural features, and living creatures. Natural obstacles obviously include e.g. rivers, swamps and mountains; while wolves, bears, elephant, rhino, crocodiles and alligators are but a few of the dangerous animals a survivor may face.

Horseshoe Bandoleer This is one of the easiest packs to make, and can be carried quite comfortably over one shoulder. To construct it you will need a square-shaped piece of material, such as a blanket. This should be laid flat upon the ground and the items to be carried placed along one edge – and padded, if necessary. The items should then be rolled within the material towards the opposite edge to form a sausage shape. The two open ends need to be tied securely, and more ties added along the length to prevent the contents shifting. The two ends can then be joined with another piece of soft material, and the pack is slung round the body.

Square Pack For this pack you will need some sort of rope or cordage. Hopefully this is already available, otherwise you may need to make some from whatever materials you have about you. Once you have this, you will be able to construct a square or wishbone frame from sticks or bamboo.

Route Selection

If you can, choose to follow a trail along a ridge rather than a route that takes you through a valley. Valley routes generally present more obstacles, such as thick undergrowth and possible river/stream crossings. Other hazards include swamps or marshy ground, which are at the best hard going and at worst, dangerous to navigate. If you have alternative routes, it is always best to detour around such areas.

Ridges also tend to provide better visibility, which will make it easier to keep your bearings. A ridge may be orientated in the direction you are travelling; more often than not, however, it is likely that the direction of the ridge will head off on a totally different bearing to the one you wish to follow. Even so, it may still be worth following the ridge for a short while, keeping an eye out for a suitable alternative route to take.

Contouring offers a useful halfway measure between ridge and valley floor. A trail that follows such a contour may take a longer route than a ridge top, but it will mean that less climbing has to be done. Without a detailed map your route selection is best made based on careful observation of the terrain.

Dig In

Fatalities involving the weather often involve some human carelessness or ignorance, both can be avoided. If the worst happens and you do find yourself and your party trapped on a hill or mountain in bad weather, find, construct or dig some form of shelter; keep together; and wait it out.

The Seasons

Apart from the need and the means to travel, a survivor must also take into account the season and the weather.

Depending on the terrain, spring can be a mixed blessing for survival travellers. For example, in the Arctic the snow will start to thaw into slush, turning the frozen tundra into an impassable bog. Spring travel through the desert or jungle will be cooler by comparison to the summer heat. There should be signs of new plant life with young roots, many of which can be eaten. Likewise, the birds will start to lay eggs and young animals will start to appear.

Summer is kinder to the survivor; the days are longer and the sun warmer, food will be readily available, and shelter easier to construct. Autumn is the survivor's most promising time, as there is a host of fresh fruit, nuts, plants and fungi; but this bounty should be harvested if you have reason to expect that you may remain unrescued for any extended period. Winter is the worst possible time to find yourself in a survival situation: cold, shortage of food sources and the most diffi-cult travel conditions all pose the greatest possible challenge.

Weather

In most survival situations long term weather factors for any ter-rain are governed by the seasons. The immediate weather is of importance, however, as it figures in decisions about travel, shel-ter-building and protective clothing. Any weather conditions to which exposure is liable to cause frostbite or heatstroke are good reasons for postponing current activity.

Although we cannot change the weather, we can to a certain extent predict its approach by observing the sky and cloud for-mations. A clear sky with high cloud will indicate a clear and sunny day; dark sky with low cloud normally indicates rain; it is simply a matter of gauging the degree between the two. Do this by looking towards the direction of travel. Try to estimate the height of cloud, colour of sky and wind direction. With a little practice you will be able to anticipate the weather conditions for several hours ahead.

Fog can be dangerous: it is disorienting, and hides dangers such as cliff edges. Where possible in these conditions, stay where you are until visibility improves. If you have to keep going then consid-er roping the members of the party together. In this way you can be assured that no one will get lost and it may also save someone from a nasty fall.

Wind gusts, especially in exposed places such as high ridge lines, can be powerful enough to knock adults off their feet. If there is any danger of this, get all party members to crawl on hands and knees and keep them close together. Again, it may be necessary to rope everyone together.

Hailstones can be up to an inch in diameter, and can fall with sufficient force to cause serious injury and damage. In the rare event of being caught out in a hailstorm, make sure you find shel-ter or at least cover your head.

Lightning It is wise to take precautions against lightning, although it is very rare for an electrical storm to occur without some advance warning, e.g. the appearance of thunderclouds in the distance fol-lowed by flashes of lightning and rumbles of thunder as the clouds approach. Be aware that lightning striking the ground normally seeks the easiest point of contact, which is usually the highest point in the area. If caught out in a lightning storm it is much safer to stay out in the open, even if in driving rain. Sit down, preferably on your rucksack, and minimize your contact points with the ground, drawing your knees up and placing your hands in your lap.

River Crossing Techniques

Sometimes when a survivor is confronted by a major watercourse there is little option other than to cross it. The width of the river, its depth and speed all pose problems, as does the type of riverbed.

Mud and silt can be extremely dangerous, to the point where you become permanently stuck or – worse – sucked below the surface. Few riverbeds are flat, and most have hidden depths into which anyone crossing may fall. Strong currents can dash the strongest of swimmers into rocky outcrops, or plunge them into falling rapids. All these obstacles must be taken into account before attempting to ford any river.

Never cross on a river bend, as the speed of the current and the depth of the water will increase from the inside of the bend to the outside. Instead, choose a wide stretch where the water is flowing slower, and where one can carefully wade across. Avoid any temptation to jump from stone to stone, as these are often slippery and a fall could result in a sprain or a fracture; at the least you may drop vital equipment. When wading across, use as many aids to safety as are available.

If you flounder or slip in the water and find yourself floating downstream, it is important not to panic. Float feet first with the current, fending off any obstacles, until you feel the river bed beneath you and are able to stand, or until you reach the safety of the bank.

Depending on the weather conditions you are advised to remove your socks and trousers before wading any river; this will allow you some increase in comfort and warmth when you dress after reaching the opposite bank. When crossing a river alone use a stout stick to provide extra stability in the water and to test ahead of you for depth, potholes and underwater obstacles.

If a rope or line is at hand and you are with a companion, make sure that the person crossing is safely secured to the bank. A survival party of three or more should follow the procedure illustrated here, which will ensure that the person crossing is always secured by at least two others.

If the water is too deep for wading and you have to swim across, make buoyancy aids. Your rucksack secured in an airtight survival bag will make an excellent floatation aid. Injured survivors should be assisted by the party linking arms around each other's shoulders, with the weakest swimmer in the middle. If necessary, place the casualty on top of a secured bouyancy aid such as several rucksacks lashed together. Move across the river with the strongest member on the upstream side,

River Tips

- Plan your route to avoid having to cross water if possible. Cross only if absolutely necessary.

- Always look for the safest crossing place. Choose the widest and shallowest stretch, and avoid bends.

- Unless in a life-threatening situation, never attempt to cross a river in flood.

- If alone, use a buoyancy aid.

- Use a safety line if available.

3-Man River Crossing

1 Make your rope into a loop. The first man can cross, inside the loop for extra safety, supported by the other two.

2 The second man can cross the river supported from both banks of the river.

3 The third man can then be helped across by the first two.

against the flow of the current; move slowly and support each other if one should stumble or fall. Take care when entering and leaving the stream, especially if the banks are steep; hold onto the bank, and help the weakest person out first.

Rafts

Rivers and their immediate surroundings contain many resources useful to the survivor. In addition to food and water, you will also find materials with which you can build a simple raft. Forget any ideas about constructing a canoe – it takes skill and a great deal of time, and requires special resources such as resin for water-proofing. However, making a raft is within everyone's capabilities. Rafts can be built with anything that has a degree of buoyancy – you do not necessarily need the luxury of old oil drums, or even timber; empty bottles tied up inside a polythene bag will serve you well. If using wood, choose a light wood such as bamboo if available.

Once your raft has been constructed, ensure that all your supplies and equipment are firmly secured to it in case the raft tips over.

Floatation Aids

❶ Foliage wrapped in tarpaulin will make an efficient floatation aid.

❷ Cut two lengths of good sized timber and lash them together to make an 'armchair'.

Do not attach too much weight to your person – if you fall in it may prevent you from staying afloat. To steer your craft in order to avoid any river obstacles such as rocks or rapids, use a long punting pole. Leave time at the end of each day to locate a riverbank campsite. Mosquitoes and other biting insects are liable to be a hazard close to water, so locate your camp on higher ground if possible. A higher location will also prevent problems if the river level rises quickly. This can happen without warning in a rainforest, even if there has been no rain in your locality, as rain may have fallen in the upper reaches. When you set up camp for the night, take great care that you have secured your raft, even taking it out of the water if possible. Check the raft for serviceability every morning and repair as required.

Constructing a Raft A raft is basically anything that floats with enough buoyancy to support a human being. The secret behind any good raft is its strength and durability over water; it does not have to keep your feet dry. The materials for making a raft can vary from brushwood and logs to polythene sacks and ponchos. Their construction needs little imagination and several ideas are illustrated here. Keep in mind that it is trapped air which makes a raft float.

A Poncho Raft

❶ Make a cross of two lengths of wood, place them with some foliage on the poncho/tarpaulin.

❷ Wrap into a package and secure with cord.

❸ Double wrap the pack with another square of material to make a long-lasting floatation aid.

Mountain Travel

Mountains, especially the lower slopes, offer the survivor or escapee many possibilities of shelter, food and water. Their drawbacks are that travelling may be more difficult, and the survivor may be at more risk of injury. Remember that surviving above the snow line will be very hard and even dangerous, so avoid climbing this high if you can. There are three basic rules to remember when travelling through mountains:

❶ Avoid any loose rock when climbing, and always make sure that you have three points of contact.

❷ Always make sure that it is possible to climb back down again if you need to.

❸ Stay out of snow fields, glaciers and overhanging snow.

Climbing with Rope

If you have a rope use it for both climbing and descending, it will make your travel through mountains far safer.

Climbing without Rope

If you have no rope always maintain three points of contact when climbing. Do not over stretch yourself. Face away from the rock when descending.

Movement in the Dark

There may be times when a survivor needs to move during the hours of darkness. For instance, in the Arctic winter there may be little option; but desert travel is best undertaken at night. In other situations it may be expedient to move by night to avoid the enemy, or to get a seriously injured survivor to immediate medical attention. If, for whatever reason, moving in darkness is the only option in your situation, you need to consider how to do this safely.

Being in complete darkness can be frightening; stay calm and take stock of the situation. Check that you have no source of lighting on you. If you are moving in a group, make sure that everyone stays within touching distance of the next person. If you have a rope or lifeline, rope everyone together, placing the weakest in the centre.

Unless a life really depends on it, do not try crossing a river in darkness – it is extremely dangerous. Likewise, while it is a good idea to follow a stream or river on the flat, never follow water down a steep mountainside, as it will inevitably have a waterfall somewhere. Even if the waterfall is small, it will be enough to cause injuries if you fall over in the dark.

Working in complete darkness produces what is known as night sight, a condition where the eyes adjust to the low level of available light. This will be interrupted if a torch or naked flame is used; always close one eye against bright lights. All the human senses become heightened when enveloped in darkness, and these should be used to their best advantage. However, be aware that heightened senses mean that even familiar noises may sound much louder and closer, which to some people can be unnerving. Stay calm, and talk to yourself or each other if necessary.

Prior to darkness falling, check the ground you intend to cross and memorize your route. If your memory is good it will assist in maintaining your route during the darkness. Distances can be confusing, as you will be forced to move more slowly. Try, if possible, to locate features which can be easily identified. Your sense of touch will be particularly useful when it is totally dark or when you are moving over steep and rocky ground. Again, always move downhill, using your hands as if you were a climber, keeping three points in contact with the rock at all times.

Use your hands and arms to make sure that the immediate space before you is clear of any obstacles and is secure to step on. If the ground is uneven or if there is the possibility of a dangerous drop, crawl on your hands and knees. Stop when you hear water, as this almost certainly indicates a drop of some height. Try throwing a stone and listen for the sound of it hitting earth or water; this should indicate distance and depth. If walking in a forest at night, stretching the arms out in front of the body will ward off low branches, etc.

Keeping the mouth open during darkness increases sound reception. Furthermore, whenever danger is imminent the senses often produce a tingling sensation as a warning. Learn to recognize these signs and accept them without interpretation – remember that we are, after all, only animals.

Light contrast is a good aid to night navigation. Snow-covered ground reflects any starlight and moonlight, but be aware that it also hides pitfalls below the surface. On a clear moonlit night it is possible to see for up to 100m (330ft) over open terrain. In wooded terrain there is also a contrast between the dark forest and the lighter sky; this contrast will act as guide if you are following a track through woodland – simply look up, and observe the treetop silhouette. Certain weather conditions provide a fair amount of lightning which will constantly illuminate the surrounding area, although somewhat briefly.

Local Population

The hazards of surviving in desolate terrain may seem to be over if you make contact with the indigenous people – but this may be far from true. Many travellers have found themselves held hostage for ransom, or have been imprisoned for breaking some fundamental local law. That said, there are few places on Earth where meeting up with the local people will not bring your survival situation to an end, provided that you obey some very basic rules.

Only the most hostile of environments are totally uninhabited, since both man and animals have adapted to virtually every type of terrain and conditions. The nomadic Tuareg have survived in the central Sahara, while the Inuit have eked out an existence in the Far North. Today many tribes have become engulfed by the trappings of Western civilization, but many still cling to their former ways of life. In many cases these isolated peoples will have some form of communication with the outside world; if not, then at least they will have food, water and shelter, and offer a hopeful means of repatriation.

In the event that you make contact with such a community, there are a number of basic rules to observe.

- Unless you are at death's door, wait outside their village until welcomed.

- Lay down any weapon, but do not let them take it.

- Spread out your palms to show you are unarmed before shaking hands.

- Have an escape route planned in case you have to run.

- Take any drink or food that is offered, and thank your host.

- Treat all people, customs and religions with respect.

- Explain your situation – use simple drawings in the dirt.

- Talk to the men; do not openly approach or talk to the women.

- Other than for medical reasons, don't remove clothes in public.

- Explain that you must move on as soon as possible.

- Thank them for their kindness when you leave.

Search and rescue
contingency plans come
into operation at the first
sign of trouble. This will
happen when a radio
distress call is received,
or waypoint call-in
procedures have
been missed.

All air traffic is monitored very closely, especially commercial aircraft flying on a set route. Radar and the more recent adoption of the satellite Global Positioning System mean that almost all transport vehicles, from aircraft to supertankers, can be tracked constantly to within a few metres. Consequently, aircraft that have been forced to make emergency landings or ships that are foundering at sea can usually expect rescue assistance within a matter of hours at worst. If for any reason the location is not known, then Search and Rescue (SAR) teams will be called in to make a search. The area covered will be based on the best estimate of the last known location.

How the search is carried out will be determined by the size of the area to be covered, the terrain, the weather and operational necessity. A search plan will be devised, and search patterns allocated to the aircraft. If radio communications can be established or a beacon signal is received, then a contact search will be initiated. This is designed to concentrate rescue efforts on a relatively small area, thus increasing the speed with which rescuers can get to you. Unless there is accurate knowledge of the location of the party to be rescued, it will be futile and even risky to send out search teams during the night.

The basic search patterns are as follows:

- **Area search** This involves dividing up the area into smaller areas using natural features as landmarks, giving boundaries in which individual teams are to search.
- **Sweep search** The rescue party will spread out in a line and search the area in a disciplined and organized manner.
- **Contour search** In mountainous country a contour search, spiralling around tall features and flying several times along steep valleys, allows maximum thoroughness.
- **Contact search** A search focused on a smaller area but based on the principles of the sweep search.

Signalling

Signalling is a means of communication which can take the form of shape, sound, silhouette and sight. Sound can encompass anything from shouting or blowing a whistle to using a radio, while sight can mean attracting attention by using anything from a signalling mirror to a smoking fire. The methods you choose will depend on what equipment is available and the conditions in which you find yourself. A direct link radio or satellite phone will produce rapid rescue results; by contrast, the light from a signal fire will only be seen once the search aircraft is over your location.

Signal Fires

Signal fires must be kept ready to be lit at a moment's notice. The tinder and wood must be dry. The fire is constructed so that the tinder is in the middle, ready for lighting. The aim is that once the tinder is alight all the other fuel should light easily and burn without too much effort on you part. This type of fire needs to be sheltered from the wet. If you are able, build three of these fires in a triangle, 30m (100ft) apart. Make sure that the ground around the fire is adequately cleared of vegetation so that the fire will not spread beyond its boundaries once lit. Using any oil or petrol that you may have can speed up ignition.

Your rescuers may appear at any time, so when the moment arrives remember that you need to produce contrast; to work properly the signal fire must stand out from its background. At nighttime it should produce tall, bright flames which are easily seen but in the daytime (except in Arctic winter conditions) you will need to produce more smoke than flame. White smoke works best on a clear day, and can be made by adding green or damp vegetation to a very hot fire. On a cloudy day, black smoke will be seen more easily, and can be produced by burning oil or rubber (aircraft or vehicle tyres). The most important thing is to make sure that your signal fire is going to light quickly and burn fiercely, increasing your chances of being seen and rescued.

Tree Signal Fire In many cases it will be possible to construct a signal fire using a single growing tree. Use one that is isolated or growing on the fringe of a forest. Make sure that when it is set alight the fire will not spread to the surrounding trees; clear smaller trees to isolate it if necessary. Thicken your signal tree by stripping branches from other nearby trees and interweaving them. Next

Personal Locators

There are many devices used for contacting and locating those who have become lost, and most have similar functions and operations. One example is the SARBE 6 (Search And Rescue BEacon), which is designed for use as a survival radio by civil or military aircrew. On activation the unit transmits a continuous, internationally recognized, swept-tone radio distress signal in the UHF 243Mhz 7.5kHz or VHF 121.5Mhz 3.75kHz distress frequencies. It also provides two-way voice communications between the survivor and approaching rescuers. Built-in self-test facilities allow a simple confidence check to be carried out for correct functioning of the unit and battery state.

The unit is activated by the removal of an operating pin, either manually or automatically by such functions as liferaft inflation or ejector seat operation. Simultaneous, omnidirectional transmission of both VHF and UHF signals then continues automatically for a minimum of 24 hours to facilitate detection by search aircraft or vessels or by any other land, sea or airborne installation monitoring these frequencies. Pressel switches located on the side of the unit allow the survivor to select the voice mode, permitting two-way communication with the rescuers. Voice communication is on both distress frequencies simultaneously. This mode is intended for use only when the survivor can see or hear the rescue craft. The SARBE 6 is waterproof to a depth of 10m (33 feet).

build a small fire under the base of the tree; this will act as a booster, and will be partially shielded by the wide branches at the base. This booster fire will need to ignite immediately; either have a container of combustible fuel handy, or – if available – use a salvaged aerosol can (hair spray is excellent). Your signal fire tree should be protected from the snow and rain if at all possible by covering it with a parachute or similar canvas. If nothing is available, check it daily and shake it to detach fallen snow or water.

Pyramid fire A pyramid fire needs a raised base and plenty of dry fuel. The aim of the base is to ensure quick ignition and a good air supply once alight. As with any signal fire, the fuel should be instantly combustible and stacked in a manner that allows air to permeate and feed the flames.

If you have a suitable salvaged aerosol can, half-bury this in the ground at an angle pointing upwards at the pyramid base. Have ready at hand a large flat stone heavy enough to depress the release button, and a torch made from a length of stick with rags wrapped around one end. At the first sign of rescue aircraft light the torch, put the stone on the button, and place the torch in the spray. Turn your back on the fire when you do this. Once the fire is burning well, distance yourself until the spray can is finished or has exploded.

Warning: Setting fire to aerosol spray is highly dangerous, and should only be attempted in a dire emergency.
Even in a survival situation extreme caution is advised, as the can will almost certainly explode.

Phones Although mainly restricted to land usage, the global telephone network is extensive and accessible in many remote places. New portable satellite phones are little larger than a laptop computer, and will operate in every environment. Anyone planning to travel or spend any time in regions where survival situations might occur should investigate beforehand access to all forms of telecommunications, from land lines to mobile phones.

Searching the passengers and luggage from any wrecked aircraft will produce a variety of communication equipment, which even if not operable from the present position may connect later on.

Mirrors and Heliographs Any type of mirror – the larger the better – is excellent for signalling providing you have bright sunshine conditions. It is simply a matter of

reflecting the sun's rays towards a search plane or party to attract their attention. All aircraft or vehicles carry a number of mirrors any one of which will serve as a signalling device. A more accurate method is to use a purpose-made heliograph. Modern variations of these are smaller than a computer disk, measuring just 5cm x 5cm (2in x 2in), yet they have the capacity to accurately reflect some 85% of sunlight up to a range of some 20 kilometres (12 miles). Mirrors work exceptionally well in the desert and areas where sunlight is guaranteed. Once any rescue aircraft gives definite signs of having spotted you, stop signalling – you will only dazzle the pilot.

A heliograph can be purpose-made or improvised from a vehicle mirror.

Light Light is obviously the ideal means of attracting attention at night, even after you have made radio contact. Light can be emitted from any number of sources: a naked flame, torch, strobe, camera, or flare.

Although they are extremely effective the problem with most flares and torches is that they are either limited to a single use, or are useful only for the duration of the batteries. All survival flares come with operating and safety instructions; make sure you read these before commencing any operation. Hand-held flares might be better used to ignite a larger signal fire.

Parachute and Missile Flares There are many different types of missile flare on the market. Some simply fire a glowing light which lasts a few seconds; some have a parachute attached, which will retard the flare's descent thus making it visible for longer.

Always read the instructions carefully and follow them to the letter. The important point is always to keep the flare pointing skywards. Parachute flares are one-shot devices, so make sure their use is justified. The number of flares supplied with any normal pistol is around nine.

Torches and Strobes Any torch is a bonus at night, but for signalling purposes a large, broad beam is required if any rescue aircraft is to see it. Moving the torch from left to right in a slow arc will help attract attention, as will shining it onto a reflective surface – it is not the light which the search aircraft crew will see, but the movement of light. Strobes are designed to create this effect by emitting an extremely bright pulsating light. On a clear night a strobe can be seen some 16km (10 miles) away.

Vehicle Lights Providing certain elements are still intact a good signalling light can also be generated from vehicle and aircraft lights. These lights are best aimed at a large surface, such as a flat snow surface or mountain wall, with the light being fanned to animate movement. If done properly this will create an effect that can be seen for many miles. Remember that the system is reliant on battery power; recharge if possible before it becomes too weak to fire the engine.

Camera Flash A modern camera flash also makes a good signalling device but, as with other battery-powered systems, it has a limited life and should be used sparingly. In cold climates batteries are best kept warm to maintain their performance.

Whistles and Sound Whistles have improved a great deal in recent years, and new models can be heard several kilometres away providing the air is still, or the wind is blowing in the right direction.

The main purpose of the whistle in many survival kits is to attract the attention of other survivors directly

Personal Locator Radios

• This is the survivor's best friend - but its battery life is limited. The 'beacon' setting uses least battery power.

• Reception and transmission are generally limited to line-of-sight – so don't waste the battery by leaving it switched on for long periods when you can't see or hear SAR aircraft.

• Try to use the radio from high ground.

• Transmit an SOS or Mayday at sunrise, noon and sunset. Try to transmit during a consistent time period, e.g. from the hour to 20 minutes past the hour.

• Transmit for two minutes each time, then switch off for one minute. Switch on for three minutes, then off for three minutes. Switch on for ten minutes, then off until the next transmission period. (USAF guidelines for use of standard PRC-90 radio.)

after the disaster. This is particularly so at sea, where all survivors should find a whistle attached to their life vest. On land anything that will amplify sound, such as beating a metal drum with a stick, should also be considered. If the survivor is lucky enough to have a firearm, firing a shot will also attract attention; but this should only be done if you believe a rescue party is nearby.

Warning: Never make a loud noise in snow-covered mountainous areas where avalanches may be caused.

Balloons Radar-reflective and colour-detectable balloons come in a variety of sizes. The coloured versions are primarily designed for use in the jungle. Normally constructed of bright orange polythene, they are inflated by mixing chemicals with water to produce helium gas. As the balloon fills it is raised on a line until it is above the dense forest canopy, and then tethered where it can be clearly seen by search aircraft. (The water bag and tin which are part of the kit may be employed for survival purposes.)

Radar-reflective balloons are more compact, and are more automated in their operation. Inflation is initiated by removing a safety pin; this activates a helium cartridge which fills the balloon. The balloon is tethered to the life jacket, from where it rises to around 30m (100ft), where it will remain even in strong winds for up to five days. The 10m (33ft) radar reflective signature can be detected by search vehicles up to 30km (18 miles) away.

Rescue Panels and Streamers These come in various shapes and sizes, but all provide a fluorescent marker which can be seen from the air. Panels are normally 2m x 0.5m (6.5ft x 16ins) or 2m square depending on the design. Two or three of these can be formed into various shapes which indicate your requirements and situation. Distress streamers are used in much the same way but are narrower and longer, up to 10m (33 feet). These can be spread on the ground or floated behind a liferaft.

Contrast Signals Disrupting the normal pattern of the terrain creates contrast. Do this by introducing regular shapes which do

Ground marker panels.

Shapes for Specific Ground Signals

N	Negative		
Y	Yes		
I	Have seriously injured		
X	Unable to move		

→ Have gone this way
△ It is safe to land here
SOS Save our souls

not occur naturally – circles, squares, triangles, letters or straight lines. A large circle with a minimum diameter of 3m (10ft) can be made using stones. It can also be broken or trampled-out in snow, but a trampled signal is improved by the addition of some contrasting material – earth, campfire ashes, even marker dye if a dinghy is found among the wreckage. On sand use rocks, sticks, cacti or seaweed. Choose the things which make the best contrast against the particular background surface. If air marker panels are available use these first and construct improvised signals secondly. Make any ground-to-air signals as large as possible, and add extra shapes if space, time and energy permit.

Increased contrast is gained if you incorporate brightly coloured wreckage, clothing, blankets, etc, in your signals.

Flying Signals Signals can also be hung from trees. Anything shiny or brightly coloured which is moving will be even more eye-catching. A flag pole will increase the distance over which signals can be seen from the ground. If any possible rescuers are seen or heard, use any available clothing or material as flags, and keep waving. If there is some suitable material that is not required for other uses during daylight hours, it is useful to have it ready, attached to the longest pole you can easily handle for the sake of maximum signalling movement. Two men holding a survival blanket, flag or other brightly coloured sheet can, by keeping it taut, manipulate it to show flashes of light or colour. These will catch a searcher's eye more readily than the display of a static sheet.

Ground Information Markers If you move from your location you may need to blaze a trail or leave ground markers to indicate direction of travel. It is easy to get lost or move off course, especially if no compass or map are available. To aid your progress and to make sure others can follow in your footsteps you will need to blaze a trail. This can be done either by chipping markers on tree trunks or leaving a prominent ground sign.

Trees should be cut at head height on both sides, making a single cut on the side pointing away from your last position, and two cuts on the side pointing towards your last position. This will allow others to follow and you to retrace your footsteps if the need arises. Always look back from time to time, making sure that your spacing between marked trees allows the next one to be seen from the position of the last.

A second method is to deliberately place natural items such as stones, sticks, grass, etc in such a way as to mark your direction. The distance apart is determined by the natural path you are taking. For example, if you are on a prominent path you need only mark direction changes at junctions. In a vast field of grass you will need to knot the tussocks on a regular basis, so that each one can be seen from the last.

Helicopter Rescue Procedures

Most SAR teams are organized along military lines. They are highly skilled and have access to excellent resources, including fixed-wing long range aircraft and helicopters. Most carry personnel and facilities for front line medical care. However, it would be a dangerous mistake to assume that they will always be there to get you out of danger.

Severe weather conditions can keep search aircraft grounded for hours or days. Even once you have been located helicopter crews can take a considerable amount of time assessing the problems of trying to reach you. Over rough seas or jungle terrain it is not uncommon for the pilot to make several attempts to establish a hover close enough to the casualties to be able to get a winchman or mountain rescue team to their position. Having arrived at a workable hover, the next priority is to assess the safest method of rescuing the survivors.

To ensure that no important aspect of the situation is overlooked SAR crews use a standardized system of priorities:
- Aircraft safety
- Winchman safety
- Survivor safety

Landing Areas Where possible the helicopter will land to evacuate survivors. To make this viable the survivor should do everything possible to provide a good landing pad (LP). Factors to be considered include the size of the clear area, the ground slope, the type of surface, and the direction of wind and approach. First check that the surface will support a helicopter, i.e. that it is not waterlogged ground or obstructed by large rocks, fallen trees, potholes, etc. Next, make sure that it is free of any loose debris that could be blown about by the rotor downdraft. Check the helicopter's approach path, which will be into the prevailing wind; make sure there are no tall obstructions to the rotor blades. Mark the centre of your LP with some form of marker such as an H-shape; and indicate the wind direction by improvising a wind sock or making smoke.

Rescue Strop The helicopter rescue strop is designed to facilitate the rescue of survivors. It can be used at sea or on land to lift uninjured survivors of any size with relative ease. The strop is manufactured from nylon webbing. A 'D'-ring is incorporated at each

Rescue teams are highly skilled at extracting survivors from the most inhospitable of places.

end of the strop; the centre portion is cushioned with a rubber sheet comfort pad tapered at each end and covered with polyester fabric. A sliding woggle through which the two ends of the strop pass enables the wearer to draw the strop close to his body before the ascent. A webbing handle is situated centrally on the strop at the wearer's back, to enable the winch operator in the aircraft to grasp the survivor and guide him back into the cabin.

Winching Techniques Most helicopter rescues involve lowering a crew member to assist those being winched aboard. During this double lift the survivor will be secured by the winchman and they are raised together. In certain circumstances this may not be feasible, and a one-man lift will be organized. When the helicopter is positioned into the wind a rescue strop will be lowered to the survivor, who must be conscious and uninjured. The survivor places the strop over his head with the winch cable to the front. It is adjusted under the armpits by tightening the webbing ring woggle, before signalling that he is ready.

Stretcher cases will always be supervised by a lowered crew member.

Helicopter Rescue

• Wait until the helicopter has landed, and either the pilot or a crew member has clearly indicated to you that you should come forward.

• Never approach a helicopter from the rear, or by descending down a slope – both will put you in extreme danger from the rotor blades.

• The best approach angle is on the cabin door side, from three-quarter front.

If you find yourself in a survival situation, whether by design or by accident, remember

FIVE GOLDEN RULES OF SURVIVAL

❶ Life itself is survival, all that changes is the environment or the conditions under which you live. When crossing a wilderness area or entering a dangerous environment do so properly equipped.

❷ A quick rescue is the best rescue. Use every modern aid to make others aware of your plight and location. No matter what the danger, good communications will prevent a survival situation evolving.

❸ We only need the basics. Given that you are uninjured and functioning properly, you need only air to breathe, water to drink, food to eat and shelter from the environment. However scarce, nature supplies all these elements but you cannot expect nature to change in order to accommodate your requirements. You must learn to adapt to use whatever she provides.

❹ Plan your survival. When disaster strikes think about your situation and make a plan of your basic needs. Through the practical applications of survival you will maintain hope and give hope to others. Maintain your health, care for the injured, build a fire if you are cold, eat if hungry and sleep when tired. Do not needlessly expend energy or put yourself in danger without good reason.

❺ Recognize that danger is everywhere. The cold can kill. The heat can kill. The sea can kill. Wild beasts can kill. Despondency can kill. Lack of nourishment can kill. Watch, listen, think and determine the problem – learn to survive.

Acknowledgments

The information contained in this book was researched from the world's elite survival schools, both civilian and military. The use of photography as opposed to illustrations has been adopted to indicate that the processes and methods actually work. Although the photographs are from various sources world-wide the contributions of Guy Croisiaux and Neil Devine are especially outstanding. The visit and introduction by Brig, Gen. Dato Modh Azumi bin Mohamed, to the survival school in Malacca was very much appreciated, supplying in the process some outstanding jungle photography. As always, without the skilful work of Julie Pembridge in coordinating the written material and helping this book develop, attainment would not have been possible. Finally the author would like to express his gratitude to the CEO of BCB International Ltd., Andrew Howell, through whose office many of the contributing companies and individuals were contacted for their support.

BCB International Ltd. UK
Beaufort. UK
Special Forces Survival School Malacca.
  Malaysia
International Long Range Patrol School.
  Germany
The Survival School. Belgium

The Royal Navy Survival School. UK
Director of Public Communication,
Pentagon. USA
Manchester Airport Security Training. UK
Martin Baker. UK
GQ Parachutes. UK
Marinair Holdings. Malaysia